Collected Reflections
on Catholic Womanhood

Conversations
for the
MODERN CATHOLIC WOMAN

MARNEE WEISBROD
JODY PITCHER
with contributors

Pursuit of Beauty Media

Conversations for the Modern Catholic Woman

Copyright © 2025 by Marnee Weisbrod and Jody Pitcher

ISBN 979-8-9925734-0-4 (softcover)

ISBN 979-8-9925734-2-8 (hardcover)

ISBN 979-8-9925734-1-1 (ebook)

Requests for information should be addressed to:

Marnee Weisbrod, connect@pursuitofbeautymedia.com

All Scripture quotations, unless otherwise indicated, are taken from the New American Bible, revised edition © 2010, 1991, 1986, 1970 Confraternity of Christian Doctrine, Inc., Washington, DC. All Rights Reserved.

Scripture quotations marked NIV are taken from the Holy Bible, New International Version®, NIV®. Copyright © 1973, 1978, 1984, 2011 by Biblica, Inc.® Used by permission of Zondervan. All rights reserved worldwide. www.zondervan.com The "NIV" and "New International Version" are trademarks registered in the United States Patent and Trademark Office by Biblica, Inc.®

Any Internet addresses (websites, blogs, etc.) and telephone numbers in this book are offered as a resource. They are not intended in any way to be or imply an endorsement by the publisher, nor does the publisher vouch for the content of these sites and numbers for the life of this book.

No part of this publication may be reproduced, stored in a retrieval system, or transmitted in any form or by any means—electronic, mechanical, photocopy, recording, or any other—except for brief quotations in printed reviews, without the prior permission of the publisher.

Cover Design and Interior Typesetting by Vanessa Mendozzi

Editing and proofreading by Shauna Perez

Proofreading and coaching by Ellen Gable Hrkach

*For all the women who have been
a part of my story, here is my tribute to you.*

For my unparalleled husband and supporter, Daren.

*For my very own little woman, Rosalina. May you always
know what is true, good, and beautiful.*

M. W.

*For the Blessed Mother,
who saw the woman in me and wanted it to flourish.*

*For the women who have helped me discover
my femininity throughout the years!*

*For my biggest fans: David (fiancé), Lorrie,
Jane, and Carol. I can see who I am
through your eyes with love,
tenderness, and encouragement,
even when things are messy.*

J. P.

Contents

Prologue	vii
1. Beauty and Femininity	1
2. Dating and Finding the Right Man	17
3. Marriage	33
4. Motherhood	49
5. Vocational Discernment	67
6. Work and Service	87
7. Friendships and Community	99
8. Fashion and Self-Expression	113
9. Healing Traumas and Mental Health	125
10. Healthy Living and Self-Care	145
11. God and the Catholic Church	163
12. Flourishing	179
A Woman's Prayer	197
Resources	199

Prologue

Seven years ago, Jody and I (Marnee) were finishing up our first counseling residency for our Master's degree. We were at the airport, about to head back to our respective states of Texas and Michigan. I felt this internal prompt, "You should get her number . . . you might need it." And so I, the timid introvert, asked my new friend, the bold and beautiful extrovert, "Hey, can I get your number?"

It turned out to be the beginning of a beautiful friendship.

Fast forward over the years: moving multiple times for both of us, graduating, starting our work as therapists, and experiencing a variety of dating relationships (and a marriage—mine!), the theme of being able to share experiences about Catholic womanhood with other women came up again and again. On the morning of April 19, 2024 (most of my best thinking happens right as I am waking up), the idea came to me to write a book with Jody (and as many other women as I could find) to do just that.

Over the course of writing this book, we all have had many significant life events. Births, miscarriages, an engagement (Jody!), moves, new pregnancies, new businesses, medical scares, and more. Many of these are reflected in the following pages. A *huge* thanks to our twenty-one contributors who gave their precious time and energy towards making this book what it is! Our ladies hail from Michigan, Texas, Ohio, Virginia, California, New York, Massachusetts, Florida, Kansas, New Mexico, and the Netherlands (Chiara and Sr. Holy Family!).

This book would not be possible without all of these women, particularly my good friend Jody. It would also not be possible without so many women and friendships in our lives before this book and also so many special client encounters that revealed to us the hearts of many Catholic women today.

This book would definitely not be possible without the unwavering support of my super husband, Daren. He believed in me long before I did, and that was part of how the idea could come into being at all. I hope he decides to share all of his experience and knowledge by writing a book of his own someday!

Our hope for this book is that it speaks to hearts and minds and breeds further conversation. If it taps into any of the "8 C's" of Internal Family Systems Therapy (IFS), then I would consider it a success. If it increases Clarity, Courage, Compassion, Creativity, Curiosity, Calm, Confidence, or Connectedness, I believe that means it is doing some good, for some woman, somewhere.

While the introvert in me has always avoided formal small groups like the plague, I deeply enjoy intentional conversations with others. However you prefer to do it, feel free to take this book and use it as a springboard for opening up these meaningful subjects with the women in your life and wrestle out your own thoughts and experiences as well.

The world doesn't need what women have; it needs what women are.

St. Edith Stein

We are all practicing Catholic women who love our Catholic faith. We do not desire to change or bend the tenets of the faith. We believe that the Holy Spirit and 2,000 years of tradition are wiser than we are. Where living the faith is hard, we seek understanding and humility (while acknowledging that it is hard, and sometimes the direction to take is not black and white).

We love being women. We believe being a woman is a gift and a treasure. We seek to foster our womanhood, understanding it ever more in the context of God's created design. We love other women: our sisterhood, our shared delights, and our unique insights. We seek to empower each other in light of our incredible design and capacities and in complementarity with our vocations. We seek to pass on to our daughters, nieces, goddaughters, sisters, and friends the joy and freedom of being an authentically Catholic woman.

CHAPTER 1

Beauty and Femininity

Who can find a woman of worth?
Far beyond jewels is her value.

PROVERBS 31:10

To a great extent the level of any
civilization is the level of its womanhood.

FULTON SHEEN

I believe the world will be saved by beauty.

FYODOR DOSTOEVSKY

MARNEE

What a wonderful topic! It gets me excited and inspired when I think about all the value, design, richness, and fruitfulness of what it is to be a woman. At the same time, it makes me sad and subdued when I consider the way these gifts can be experienced as sources of pain or confusion to many women around us.

Women are such a gift to the world! Famous people have noted this over time, and it has also been so affirmed by the Church, especially recently by St. John Paul II (JPII). We bring beauty into the world simply by being *woman*. We bring fruitfulness by our very design (whether we bear children or not). We bring love, relationship, empathy, connection, creativity, and home . . . just to name a few.

As much as we women can connect to our deepest selves and delight in the lovely garden God has created that is us, it is an even more amazing experience to try to see woman through the eyes of man. And especially *her* man. For it is part of the mystery of man and woman being made for each other that the one is only truly known and valued when beheld by the other. What it means to be a woman can perhaps be most profoundly articulated by her complete compliment, her manly spouse. And likewise, when we behold our man, we can know manhood in a way man himself may not conceive of.

Upon further reflection, this reminds me of when Adam was presented with Eve. He beheld her and could immediately bestow her name. He had never conceived of her before, but when he was in her presence, he knew "woman."

We can dismiss many of the cliche labels for women of old, as well as the modern descriptors for women of today. We don't need to play to liberals or conservatives, and we don't need to get hung up on terms and their modern interpretations. Today, language is a confused mess. So many words that would help explain and discuss important concepts have been labeled judgmental to justify censorship. Words that were meant to express reality are now called oppressive or restrictive and feed wars of agenda.

Let's step back from all this anger and contention and simply revel in who we are, in the joy of our womanhood. We are strong and smart, we are loving and patient, we are deep and giving, we are practical and protective, we empower our men and carry our children. We love to serve and facilitate the growth of those in our care. We endure much pain, and we suffer personal frustrations and disappointments. We are the muses of art and literature and have changed the course of nations and culture. We live humbly, work hard, and feel satisfied with a good day's work. See how great our capacity and how varied our gifts. We bring beauty and newness wherever we go, without effort, because it is who we are.

The world was incomplete without us, and some would say we are the pinnacle of creation (especially our men), because we were the final, finishing touch on God's creative work. What does God have in store for our lives with all these lavish gifts he has given us? At some point, many of us will have to take our gifts and potential to deep prayer and reflection. Perhaps for years.

Most of us come to understand true femininity and beauty slowly over our adult years. Wading through many messages, attuning our ears carefully to truth, allows us to glean the various fragments and assemble them together.

But we women know what it is to care for, nurture, and grow life within ourselves, slowly, patiently, over time. We know the seed begins very small, even invisible, but with careful tending, it becomes an immeasurable gift that brings life to all. Here is a blog excerpt from Carrie Gress that I find expresses this womanly reality so well:

> While it is perfectly clear that men and women differ physically, there is another difference that may not always be so apparent: in women's spiritual lives and the way God communicates with us . . .
>
> Often there will be a time in a holy woman's life when she says something like, "The Lord put this on my heart. I spent years praying for it, struggling with it, and eventually it all came together in a more beautiful way than I could have imagined." In a way analogous to physical childbearing, God will often plant a seed within a woman's heart that is known only to her. Over time, she will nourish the seed as it grows, until it comes to the fullness of reality. Like giving birth to a baby, spiritual growth is a very interior experience of first knowing, then growing, then finally realizing the fullness of God's plan.
>
> Women have been made for a deep interior life, to dwell in the "living water" of Christ. God speaks to us there and plants the seeds that, with our cooperation, he will one day bring to fruition. And yet none of it can happen if a woman never finds silence.
>
> Edith Stein said that women collect their forces in silence. It is important for husbands to understand this unique relationship and to help their wives carve out swaths of silence in their busy schedules. Without it, the entire life of the family will lack the critical foundation that comes from a woman's deep connection to God.

So, we likewise take our wounds, our questions, and our confusion to this place of deep reflection and allow God, good woman friends, our spouse, and other truth-speakers to help us journey to the place to freely and abundantly rejoice in our beauty and femininity.

JODY

Some readers might remember hearing from their mother (or as an implicit message), "You don't need a man," or "Be independent" or "Don't depend on a man to be there." I prided myself on being self-reliant, independent, and not needing a man for anything. However, that lie was challenged when I got divorced. Since 2015, I have learned what real femininity is, what it is not, and how beauty is the fruit of our femininity.

So, what does femininity mean to me? It is the individual uniqueness of our nature to receive and give life through our hearts. We are all created differently, and we as women should celebrate that. I am a tomboy, so my femininity will show up differently than a woman who is more girly. It doesn't make either wrong, just different.

What we share in our femininity is how our hearts are created. A woman's emotions contribute to her relational nature. The Blessed Mother gives us the example of how to allow our hearts to be open without protecting ourselves. She allows the Lord and St. Joseph to protect her in order for her heart to deal with the joys and pains of this world. And boy, did she have joys and pains!!

When the Blessed Mother gives her fiat, twice, explicitly, in a big way (and we can assume daily), she says yes to God's authority over her life. She trusts that God has her ultimate good in mind.

With that goodness, God presents to her his mission for her, and she accepts it. She *submits* to *him*!! I said it . . . *submit*. Ladies, we can submit to a man's authority *if* we believe in the mission that he presents, which includes his relationship with the Lord.

The feminine heart is to be protected and not on defense *all* the time. I was a woman who couldn't allow my needs, sorrows, or pain to be seen. I would swallow it and keep moving forward because I needed to be strong. This led to my heart slowly becoming calloused, stressed, and frustrated with life. I was starting to feel disconnected from my femininity and began tapping more into my masculine side. Protecting myself from the world due to my wounds was chipping away at my creation, which meant I wasn't flourishing—until God revealed his heart to me.

Our femininity showcases our purpose—to cultivate life in the world. Femininity can't be a box to put a woman in. Through my healing, I had to understand that my femininity is needed in the world and not a mistake. I had to learn how to accept and embrace characteristics of women that others would say were wrong.

God needs a woman who is direct, decisive, orderly, proactive, outspoken, outgoing, not shy to stand up for what she believes, a woman who has clear expectations, practices structure with flexibility, makes things happen, tackles conflicts, and brings people together. I know how to have fun, be comforting, compassionate, nurturing, and not take things too seriously. I don't paint my nails, buy accessories, or like to go shopping. That doesn't mean I am not feminine. But when I would see others be more gentle and soft, it would cause me to think there was something wrong with me. (I am only speaking from my experiences and understand that there are women who are the opposite and have the same struggle in reverse.)

My point is that God created each of us intentionally, and it is natural that our femininity will look different. Embrace your femininity, however that looks, and know that you are needed in the world as the woman you were created to be. The world wants you to believe the lie that you need to be more like a man to survive. While that may be a driving force in today's society, that is a lie from the enemy to destroy one of the most sacred creations, the *woman*.

THE CONVERSATION CONTINUES

The devil hates beauty and femininity, and he is working hard to disfigure both. As a young teenager, I almost fell for his lies. I grew up loving sports and the outdoors, and most of my friends were boys. I used to compare myself to other girls and thought I lacked something—that I wasn't beautiful enough, feminine enough.

Once I started to bring all this to prayer, Christ reminded me of the true meaning of beauty and femininity: loving him and loving others as I am called to. I became passionate about true beauty and authentic femininity, and I realized both grow with holiness. The world needs our beauty and our femininity. The world needs us to be holy.

Vicky T.

I was always told that Mary was the most beautiful woman who ever lived. When I was in high school and through most of my twenties, however, I could not fathom that God wanted me, a clumsy, chubby, loud-mouthed, stubborn Asian girl, to see Mary as my role model.

I thought that imitating Mary would mean giving up parts of my personality and desires. The Mary that I had grown up learning about was graceful and docile. She was beautifully simple and simply beautiful. If she was the epitome of all women, then I thought that any version of femininity had to look like this.

As my relationship with the Lord continued over the years, I could feel Jesus continue to gently nudge me towards his mother. "Jesus, I love you, but I am nothing like her. I am so sorry," I would whine back.

After years of his gentle pursuit of my stubborn heart, I suddenly felt a pull to begin praying the Rosary daily and to set it as a priority. Mary began to introduce me to herself. In particular, she guided me through her experience when she and St. Joseph lost Jesus on their trip back from Jerusalem. I reflected on how frazzled Mary must have looked searching for Jesus. I contemplated her desperation and pain at losing him and how frantic she was to find him. Unlike my initial perception of femininity, Mary did not daintily prance around until she found Jesus. She was in pain, she was dirty and sweaty, and she was most likely shouting—not gently calling for Jesus in her customer service voice.

Mary was without sin, but she was not perfect. She was human. In calling us to live out our feminine genius, God is not reducing us to dainty little flowers. Instead, God's gift of our femininity calls us to be present and in pursuit of the Lord. Exercising our femininity means calling to mind our strengths in productivity, nurturing, and action. I used to think that if Mary was what God considered beautiful, then I would certainly not be enough for him, but this is certainly not the case! Embracing and acting on the gifts that God has given us, both individually and as women collectively, is our femininity, and our femininity in action is the most beautiful thing we could give to God.

Angie E.

Loving oneself, especially physically as a woman, is a constant, lifelong battle. I think my largest downfall was assuming that one day it will "just happen"—that I will just suddenly love myself, and that will be the end of it. But now, roughly twenty-odd years into the battle, I'm still not seeing any lights at the end of the tunnel. I often sit with friends and even my mom, and we talk about loving ourselves and just "wearing it anyway" or telling each other, "You look fine!"

The truth of the matter is that, in speaking of loving ourselves, it's often more of a persuasion tactic. Maybe if we say the words out loud often enough, they will become so ingrained that they become the truth. Maybe one day we won't need the words anymore. It's exhausting.

I think we need a massive paradigm shift. As a wife, mother, busy student, etc., we likely have to choose between fitness, making a healthy meal, keeping up the house, or participating in a hobby you actually *enjoy* (I'm not a fan of workouts!). I remember in a recent conversation with a friend, we were talking about weight (naturally), and I finally said, "I can't do art *and* be skinny! There simply isn't enough time."

We need to learn to operate differently—see ourselves differently. Is it our bodies that make us beautiful? Our empathy or perceptiveness? What about our contribution to life? Or art? I think the answer is somewhere between the lines!

Beauty comes from how we surround ourselves and how we let it filter through us. Maybe we aren't the beautiful thing itself—beauty shouldn't try to be caged within our bodies or stopped at the physical plane. We must be the *conduits* for beauty. It needs to flow through us and into the world. I truly believe this means something different for every woman.

Raechel W.

There is a popular quote that perfectly sums up what many of us discover all too late in life: "True beauty emanates from a woman who boldly and unabashedly knows who she is in Christ." The irony is that we uncover authentic beauty in ourselves more deeply as our earthly beauty begins to fade.

Mother Teresa is a wonderful example of this beauty stemming from identity; each wrinkle and each laugh line encapsulated a beauty the world cannot comprehend. I used to hear people say how she was a true beauty, and I would nod in agreement and respond from a pseudo-self and say, "Oh yes, look how beautiful!" but interiorly I was trying to remember the name of the expensive Beverly Hills wrinkle cream that I kept seeing flash on my Instagram feed. I think $97 to erase wrinkles is a fair deal! I had a gnawing sense that I would learn to see her aged face as physically beautiful, but I first needed an internal beauty makeover. That beauty makeover was only found in the salon chair of identity restoration. My journey through my 40s was the greatest gift of aging, heartbreak, youthful vigor, and surrender.

Entering my 50th year, I still lack the credibility to speak with authority on this; I am a baby entering the second half of my life, but I enter it with new eyes. Somewhere in my early 40s, as the Lord began to pursue my heart more passionately, I distinctly remember one moment of being drawn into the small wrinkles around the eyes and mouths of other women and thinking, "Gosh, a maturing woman is so much more attractive, why is that?" The cream Beverly Hills MD was trying to sell me was fake, tempting me to miss out on this. I needed to see with alternate eyes, a different perspective. As my identity in the Lord grew, I began to embrace who I am, both the darkness and the light, the new skin and the scars and the wrinkles, and embrace how Jesus feels for me. The outcome was a mind-shift, seeing with the eyes of the Beloved.

St John Paul the Great, in writing *Mulieris Dignitatem,* speaks about the Feminine Genius, which encompasses four unique aspects: receptivity, sensitivity, generosity, and maternity. I want to highlight receptivity as it seems to be the entry point for all other aspects.

Looking at what receptivity is not, we can look back at the creation story in Genesis. Eve, doubting her heavenly Father, chooses to grasp for what she wants as she clutches the apple. I can see the many places I've grasped at apples or idols: maybe relationships, false ideas, or a bottle of Beverly Hills MD wrinkle cream. When I choose to take care of my needs through self-reliance and I doubt that the Father will fill me, I grasp at the apple all over again. Grasping is not receptivity.

Another example of what receptivity is not: when I look toward Adam, perhaps still holding the apple, he swallows quickly when God finds him in the garden...busted!!! I imagine Adam dropping the apple, maybe even kicking it in Eve's direction as he exclaims, "It was the woman who gave me the apple." He turns away, he even blames. At times, I grasp for the apple like Eve, but sometimes, like Adam, I refuse even to hold the things in my life, preferring to close off, to stay guarded, and play it safe. I choose not to believe God can work in and through me. Maybe I close off from a new friend because I am afraid to be hurt again, or I lie about my needs or mute my feelings to protect from that crippling ache of desire. Refusal to hold or feel is not receptivity.

Receptivity is best seen in the image of the Pietà. Mary, who comes as the New Eve, shows us the way of a woman's feminine beauty. In the Pietà, we see the open heart and open hands; Mary's one hand cradling the body of her dead son. Unafraid to die with him, she stays with him in the pain - open, receptive. Mary's other hand is fully open to God, a surrender to give back to the Father and to receive from him. Learning to stay in this receptive posture takes some pretty tough mother skills, and the only one who can show me to be receptive in this way is Our Lady. I often meditate on this image to help me stay grounded in a secure identity, neither clutching nor dropping, staying open, knowing who I am and who I belong to. I have never found anything more attractive than this, and I've never felt more beautiful than I do now, both inside and out. It is the secret elixir to Mother Teresa's wrinkles. I invite you into this way of receptivity and beauty.

Eileen W.

CHAPTER TWO

Dating and Finding the Right Man

I ADJURE YOU, DAUGHTERS OF JERUSALEM,
DO NOT AWAKEN OR STIR UP LOVE
UNTIL IT IS READY!

SONG OF SONGS 8:4

SHE SEEKS OUT WOOL AND FLAX
AND WEAVES WITH SKILLFUL HANDS.

PROVERBS 31:13

MARNEE

Oh boy (no pun intended)! This is a loaded topic to me. Honestly, aside from working through childhood wounds, I think dating and waiting for the right man was the hardest experience of my life. I still have recurring dreams about being in that place of meeting guys and wondering, "Where is the right man?" or "Is this him?" even though I have been happily married for over three years!

Since I was thirteen, I knew I desired marriage and motherhood and was convinced I'd be married by the age of twenty-three and have ten kids. Sounds like the dream, right? All I wanted was to be barefoot and pregnant in the kitchen. Really, that is still my dream life, and now I have it (with one perfect kid, instead of ten). I am, in fact, barefoot so often that most people comment on it. A landlady in NYC found it so unusual living in the Bronx that she called me the Barefoot Contessa. And now, my little daughter kicks off her shoes every chance she gets. But I digress.

So, I did not get married at twenty-three. Twenty-three came and went. And then twenty-four, twenty-five, twenty-seven, twenty-nine, thirty, thirty-two . . . and each new year felt excruciating at times. Especially with the heartbreaks and emotional roller coasters of dating men who, while good men at heart, were usually burdened by their own wounds and immaturities, making for unstable or hurtful experiences. If someone had told me at twenty-three that I'd wait another twelve years before I'd get married, I may have, in true damsel form, fainted and never recovered. "Bring the smelling salts!"

Now, my husband is an absolute dream. He seriously defies all those years of idealistic expectations that only a true melancholic can create. Yet, it has still been a long, slow process to heal the deep hurt, loss, and disappointment of the previous years. Based on the recurring dreams, there may be some PTSD in there somewhere, too. And really, the hurt part is usually more about God than the men. I can be relieved I did not marry men who were not suited for me, but what in the world was God's excuse for allowing these experiences to happen to me?

For a Catholic woman, life circumstances can often feel like God is directly doing all things *to* you, or you might adopt the similarly distorted narratives: "God allowed this to happen so that . . . " or "God knew I needed that [hard, hurtful] thing to happen so that . . . " Such beliefs feed into the same concept around hurt and loss that God is responsible for or wanted or was, at the very least, okay with it.

I don't know about you, but I had to get to the point that I stopped framing God in that way, or I always just ended up with a sadistic God who needed to hurt me (or let me be hurt) so that I learned something. What kind of parent is that? Eventually, I learned to reframe it with a perspective of God that felt far more accurate and consistent: bad things happen because we've collectively brought brokenness in the world. They happen to all, without discrimination. Let's be honest; sometimes they happen even more to the faithful Christian. But God is here, he is near, and he desires to redeem each bad thing that happens. He is the one that brings the good out afterwards, as fast as he can.

So, I experienced lots of perceived hurt from God and lots of confused feelings over the years of dating and waiting. Now, he did ultimately give me the treasure, and life has been so positive because of the many years my husband and I both individually sorted through our "stuff" before getting married, but it was still hard to let go of the sense of entitlement and the resentment towards God. If I am faithful, don't I deserve to get things the way I want? I think I have a pretty good sense of God's will, 'cause we are pretty tight, and I'm not far from perfection over here (if I do say so myself). So, why is this big thing still not happening?

This journey is not one for which I can write a guidebook. Though, if I may, I hope I can ease some fears and common pressures:

1. You don't have to turn yourself into someone else to find the right man. Not at all. Introvert here! I can't say how many times I was told "you need to get out more," "you need to be more open," "you need to be more social," "you need to give it a chance, you never know . . ." No, gracias. None of that actually made a difference in helping me find a husband. (And, ironically, somehow I got a very extroverted, sanguine, people-loving spouse. And it's great.)
2. It's not about what prayers you say, when, or to whom. Breathe! Gosh, there are so many pressures for this in Catholic circles. One of the worst is, "If you haven't found your husband yet, you haven't been praying for him enough!" Oh. My. Word. Don't even get me started. God is not a vending machine.

Let me refrain from writing volumes on this topic and say a couple of things. I found it difficult to impossible to pray for my future spouse for nearly all of my adulthood. So, I didn't. And he still came. Don't beat yourself up on this one. You'd have to try really hard to mess up God's plan. He's powerful and omniscient.

When I met my husband, I was so disillusioned with men, dating, God's involvement, etc., that I met him during a spiritual low point, dealing with more hurt and confusion with God than consolidation and enlightenment. (I will say, though, my one spiritually consistent buddy was St. Joseph. And I was ultimately married on his feast!)

This may be a bit tangential, but it seems a point relevant to other women I've encountered. I found that when the time came, at thirty-four years old, after many years of heartbreaking singleness, pulling myself up by my bootstraps, providing for myself, making hundreds of practical life-survival decisions I never wanted to make on my own . . . when the time came to make the symbolic change of moving out of singleness and into a life joined to my husband . . . I was emotionally breaking down! Why?? For a moment, it felt like an almost impossible hurdle, and I didn't even know what it was. Hadn't I been hoping, praying, planning, and waiting for this day? When I came to this juncture, I just kept crying and couldn't get myself to pack up.

After conversations and reflections, I realized that all of those experiences I listed above, which made singlehood so hard and disappointing, were also the reality of me pouring my blood, sweat, and tears into building my life. I had to. I didn't want to. But I did it. And now I was being asked to give up that life. To put myself out in the most vulnerable way in sharing my life with another and even beginning to *rely* on him to provide, take care of, support . . . it was just a very surprisingly rough transition. But it was brief, and once it was made, the life I had hoped for unfolded smoothly. There was still the next wave of transition and separation when it came to the idea that I did not *need* to find any and all employment to fill my time in order to support myself. I could finally begin to let go and allow my husband to take on the primary role in that burden, which I had never wanted to have anyway.

But, each part of the journey is important. As life unfolded, the education, experience, and expertise I had built during singlehood would end up being essential in the early years of marriage to allow us to build towards the future we wanted. It was all oriented towards the goals I had recognized at thirteen years old; they just had so many different pieces along the way that I never could have anticipated.

JODY

Strap in for the ride!! It's going to be bumpy, rough, and leave you with scars, bruises, and lots of tears and confusion. And then one day, it happens. "It" not being "Oh, I found the one, and now everything is blissful" but more like flourishing while being in the desert.

Dating, finding the "right" man, marriage, children... dreams, expectations, and the "ideal" life we all have when we are young are themes and desires very deep and personal to each of us. I knew since I was ten years old that I desired to be a wife. Yep, just a wife. The children aspect was not on the radar. I assumed that would come naturally as fruits from the marriage (more on that later).

I didn't have guidance on how to date properly or in a healthy way. I had limited exposure to a faith life growing up. I didn't know the proper stages of courtship, intentional dating, or why waiting to have sex until after marriage was important. I was not protected in that way, so I made decisions based on the information I had: *public school sex ed*. What a way to destroy the goodness and sacredness of a woman.

I *never* liked the dating process!!! The peacock shows you his feathers, and you may like them, but it wasn't a guarantee that things would work out or be healthy. I was a tomboy, and in consequence, the boys liked me as one of them but not one to date (the tomboy in me wasn't attractive to most boys). I didn't have very many prospects, and that was devastating.

I felt like there was something wrong with me. All my friends would have guys chasing them a lot, but the guys were few and far between for me. This pattern instilled the fear that I would never find someone, so best to go with the ones that at least pursued me. This negative belief I held without knowing it led me to make a huge mistake when I married my ex-husband.

So here is where the ride started . . . I started with having a distorted understanding of what love was after my father left and my mother remarried. Thirty-five years ago, dating looked like this: boy sees girl, boy approaches girl, girl decides if she likes him, and they start a committed relationship. Simple right??? Heck, NO!

Now, dating in my forties is a nightmare. Ghosting, friends with benefits, "let's not define it," situationships, women pursuing the men, women not requiring the men to step up, etc. *What planet am I on????* I was married for sixteen years, and we were together for twenty-one by the time the divorce was completed. Going into the dating world has been like flying off a cliff without a parachute.

On top of that, being in your forties and applying boundaries around sex weeds out a lot of boys and leaves you lonely. Yes, boys. Ladies, keep that bar at a reasonable height, and the right man will step up and reach it or even excel over it. Let him be the *man* so you can be the *woman*. Teach them how you want to be treated, and they will follow through or they will leave. Don't be afraid of them walking away.

You will hear or might have heard from men, "Your standards are too high," or " You'll be waiting a long time if you don't have sex before marriage. No one will wait." To translate, these men are saying: "I am not self-aware, I'm emotionally unavailable, and I don't practice self-control. I don't have the virtues to be your man."

Your response: "That's too bad. I wish you the best." Smile and walk away with your head held high. Then gather your girlfriends, get some good ice cream, and talk about how God just helped you get one step closer to your man. Praise God!!!

Dating and finding the right man at any age first starts with *you*. I had to learn that my wounds led me down a path where I dated two men that were not a good fit, and ultimately, I married the second one. My wounds explained away the red flags and kept me in situations longer than I needed to be in them. I would make a bouquet of red flags, run towards the fire, and rationalize it all with the *mis*understanding that if I didn't take this opportunity now, it would never happen for me.

The enemy likes to instill fear, which manifests as feelings of scarcity, urgency, and pressure. You don't have to have it all together or all your wounds healed (they won't be on this side of heaven anyway) or even understand what God is doing or why you are in the desert.

Find your place in the uncomfortable where you can ask yourself, "Who am I doing this for?" and "What am I doing this for?" instead of "Why is this happening to me?" or "Why will God not bring me a man?"

Why, why, why . . . ? The why gets us stuck in a pattern with God with an anxious heart. Of course, it's okay to ask the why, but know that asking the who and what is more relational and can lead you to a deeper and more mature relationship with the Lord, which will flow into your future spouse.

I have so much to say about this topic, so I'll leave it here for now. I hope that you can find a place of feeling grounded, safe, and secure in the uncomfortable season of singlehood, dating, and finding the right man. Just remember, the "right man" is on the cross, and he will show you what the right man looks like.

THE CONVERSATION CONTINUES

First, I had to work on my own character and grow in virtue. Then I asked, "How free is he to love?" That question summed up a lot of my wish list qualities when I was dating. Is he free from addictions (even small addictions like the cell phone/games/etc.), and does he have a heart striving for God? Finding the right man for me meant finding a man who wanted to be holy and was excited to be a father. It also meant finding a man who had the same vision for marriage and family life as I did.

Vicky T.

Keep watch that you do not become unhealthily attached to the person you are dating.

I have wasted too much time in relationships that I should not have stayed in. Now, my biggest advice with dating is to be authentic, honest, and chaste. These things will help you keep a healthy perspective while dating.

Some of you may be familiar with the "Healing the Whole Person" retreat by the John Paul II Healing Center. I went to this retreat a few years back, and it was very enlightening for these "stuck" relationships I found myself in. I realized my wound from my parents' divorce caused me to vow to never get divorced. Now, this may sound good, like a wanted outcome of my life! However, this vow made from fear was binding me in an unhealthy way to my relationships. I found that I didn't really want to make the commitment of marriage because of the possibility of divorce. On the other hand, I would never break up with the person I was dating because that also felt like a divorce—I was already too attached to the person to let go when I should have.

Realizing the root of my behavior was so helpful. The prayer and counseling that commenced after this realization helped me break free from this pattern.

You must be ready to do the will of God no matter what that is. Break up with someone, marry that someone. Check yourself along the path of discernment. Are you being honest? Like, really honest? What vows might you have made from a wound? What is the voice of God saying? Trust it! And move forward grounded in who God made you. You will be unhappy if you do not listen to his voice.

Claire H.

I was always interested in the most interesting man in the room. I was drawn to people with large personalities or charismatic traits. From the time I was in high school, dating was always about marriage for me. In my daydreams, I would get married around twenty-four, have a child in the next couple years and build a small family. However, as I approached twenty-four and eventually passed it, that dream morphed and took on different facets.

I continually found myself drawn to men who were bright in personality or talent. Most of them were honestly great. However, it seemed the common thread that often led to the relationships' demise was a lack of interest or readiness for commitment. Granted, I have my own flaws and shortcomings that contributed to the issues. But what I found at the end of the day was that real attractiveness, for me, came in balancing my own traits.

I was bubbly, chatty, and passionate—sometimes feisty. As one friend once said, "Every relationship needs a ground and a sky." I knew that I could operate as "the ground" but truly in my heart, I wanted to be "the sky."

When I finally quieted the rom-coms and fantasy novel storylines in my head, I found that the beating heart of my desire was someone who could be steady when I waivered—someone who would laugh with me (and yes, at me) but also give me space to be as silly or passionate as I needed to be. I desired a leader in kindness and faith.

God's whisper is so powerful, but we also need to be still to hear it. When my ears finally opened, the man standing in front of me was the opposite of everything I had thought I wanted and in the best ways possible. Where anxiety had always dominated my relationships, I suddenly found an almost alarming lack of noise. It felt . . . simple. It's so important to not only be open to our desires but also to the possibility that the best thing for us is not always the immediately obvious path. That path is worth the wait, whether you're twenty-four or forty-four!

Raechel W.

Instead of fully enjoying the grandeur of my early twenties, I often found myself caught up in an exhausting, turbulent headspace when it came to the ebb and flow of the young adult dating scene. In addition to doubts that prospects would ever pan out, I was faced with the dilemma of how to establish enough of a relationship with a male stranger to know if I was interested in dating him at all!

Attempts by the woman always seemed to be perceived as intense interest, coming on too strong, or taking too much of the lead. What was I to do, then, when there was no real semblance of pursuit, when faced with a staggering majority in my social circles of "guys" as opposed to "men"? Repeated scenarios would come up, along with the same spiraling questions that sounded like a broken record.

The change that made a difference did not come from new circumstances or better prospects. Rather, a change in my interior life shook off this pattern and opened the door to a new chapter. The basis for this change was ultimately growing my relationship with God the Father. In developing my personal relationship with him, I came to trust that he would make good whatever I gave to him—all my earnest efforts and however many years of continued "singleness." With that knowledge in my heart, I was able to better receive his gifts to me. I began investing in my talents, flourishing where I was at, dialing into the now, and enjoying the adventure before me. I called this "embracing the question mark."

Looking back, this pivotal time formed me into a healthy individual ready to meet her equal. My desire for marriage matured from impatience to a mature longing no longer tied to FOMO (fear of missing out) and anxiety about finding a partner. I could hope without losing my peace. I experienced a tremendous degree of growth, healing, and happiness over the course of two rich years of young adult life.

As a result, when the man who is now my husband appeared on the scene, we encountered one another as friends with similar values, interests, and a maturity that allowed us to connect on a deeper level than any friendship before. This ability to walk alongside one another, so prepared to receive and rejoice in one another, resulted from first developing a relationship with God and coming to know the way that he desired for me to be joyful and enriched as much at the starting line as when entering into a serious relationship.

Elizabeth P.

CHAPTER THREE

Marriage

> Her husband trusts her judgment;
> he does not lack income.
>
> She brings him profit, not loss,
> all the days of her life.
>
> **PROVERBS 31:11–12**

> When a man loves a woman, he has to become worthy of her. The higher her virtue, the more noble her character, the more devoted she is to truth, justice, goodness, the more a man has to aspire to be worthy of her.
>
> **FULTON J. SHEEN**

MARNEE

While the path to get here was long and very hard at times, marriage has been an amazing gift. We are daily reminded that we did not merit each other, we were not entitled to each other, but to receive another person is a tremendous gift that can only come from a good God.

During the dating years, it seemed everyone was constantly warning us how hard marriage would be and to not be too picky when it comes to our spouse. Honestly, it's pretty terrifying to imagine what marriage would be like if I had taken that advice. Thankfully, God intervened many times to keep me from walking down the aisle with someone less than ideal for me. (As much as I was kicking and screaming against his intervention each time.)

Truly, I did want to marry a great man who amazed me; I just didn't think I deserved one or that one would want me. Whatever form it ultimately took, waiting (thirty-three years!) to meet the man beyond my dreams was the best life decision I could have made. Well, maybe I can't take full credit for that "decision" (recall the kicking and screaming). But I do have vivid memories of being a child in the early years of reason and, recognizing my own stubbornness, asking God to make sure I stayed on the right path even if I put up a big fight every time I didn't want to . . .

Another good decision was trying to make the most of my life as it was, in the state it was in, and putting in lots of work to get to know myself and resolve wounds as they appeared. I don't truly regret many things, but I do kind of wish I had been humble enough to start therapy sooner than I did.

What are some of the things that make marriage wonderful? The glory of being a real man and a real woman. Those who know,

know. And those who don't yet, hopefully will. God's design for our nature is a wonderful thing! It sure takes a lot of work to discover and cultivate our authentic femininity and masculinity, but the more you do, the more it brings life. And in this case, that is not just a metaphor. That's how real the experience can be (babies!).

Marriage brings a partner in all things. Companionship, accountability, support, insight, challenge, opportunity, dynamism, and so much more. It still makes my heart a little sore that certain communications within the Church speak about marriage as something "lesser" in the "big V" vocational rankings or as a state of life that necessitates a "divided heart" towards God. I don't fully know where these terms and ideas came from, but I know they can be wielded today by consecrated groups seeking recruits, priests who are a bit too far removed from the lives of the lay faithful, or married persons who have become disillusioned with their vocation.

Slowly, these messages may be evolving towards truth in the Church. Perhaps because there are a growing number of canonized married saints. I can almost feel the collective sigh of relief and exclamation of tentative hope from married people across the ages: "See! Married people can be saints too!"

So, no settling. Marriage will have its challenges, so why make it harder? Please let go of that terrifying thought in the back of your mind "But what if there is no one after him?" about the man you are dating. Trust me. Likely, what is even more terrible than breaking up with him is what happens when you marry him motivated by this fear.

It can be a very sweet thing to have another person to put before yourself and to work on loving. The vocation and sacrament of marriage gives that deeper meaning to your life in such a way that putting your dishes into the dishwasher instead of the sink or waiting until the baby wakes up to mow the lawn in order to serve the needs of your spouse can be deeply satisfying and life-giving. In times past, there was a certain image of the Catholic married couple where the man was noticeably dominant and authoritative, and the wife was markedly submissive and reserved. A misunderstanding of Scripture has led to a lot of hurt and distortion of masculinity and femininity. It was no surprise (though still very sad) to enter the mental health world and find how prevalent narcissism can be among Christian married men.

Times are evolving, and I believe that with the slow spread of a better understanding of Scripture, mental health awareness, and women's changing views of themselves, these household dynamics are decreasing. But how easy it is for the pendulum to simply swing in the opposite direction! We do have a hard time with balance and navigating the mushy middle as humans.

Neither husband nor wife is meant to dominate the other. It is not the love and sacrifice I am talking about to put yourself into the position of being controlled, used, manipulated, or kept down. I know many find themselves in those positions and did not intend to be there. Sometimes, as we grow and heal, our understanding of what we deserve changes. That can put us in a difficult position of finding out later we are not being treated as we deserve. That is not quite the scope of this chapter, but if you find yourself in this position, please reach out for help and support to get good guidance and healing for yourself, and if possible, your spouse and marriage.

It is amazing that we so rarely encounter truly healthy marriages. As a result, we often don't even know how marriages are supposed to operate! I am grateful to have spent a few months living with a happily married couple several years ago, which showed me in an up-close way that a good marriage is indeed at least possible.

For my husband and me, I am often astonished at the types of expectations and sayings I had adhered to in preparation for marriage. For instance, I held the idea that I had to be prepared to hand over all final decisions to my husband as the sign of the husband being head of the household. In actual married life, I find that both impractical and unrealistic. Essentially, if that were the formula, we'd have to sit down, discuss our thoughts on a subject, and then I would have to simply stop talking and ask him to make a pronouncement on the verdict. That just isn't how conversations work, and I don't think either of us would even enjoy the process.

In our decision-making, we respect and trust each other. Sometimes one of us has stronger feelings about something; sometimes the other does; sometimes we just decide what is most practical. We benefit greatly from having different perspectives and experiences in order to form our mutual decisions. If we are not in agreement or neither one has stronger feelings/knowledge on the subject, we table it for the moment and take more time for thought.

And then there is money. What a trigger-happy subject! I'm pretty sure we all have money wounds in some form or another. Money and family of origin, I think, are often the most sensitive subjects to address in marriage. Just watch how you react and how defensive you get if certain subjects are brought up.

When it comes to money, my husband and I have also found our system to be one of respect and trust. Assets are shared, and we consult each other on financial decisions large and small. Again, if one has stronger feelings about a purchase, we take that into account. It doesn't matter who is making what money; the significance of work has more to do with time allotment and what roles work best for our family. Talking about money can be a minefield at times, but we keep talking about it patiently (this is after years of self-work and individual therapy prior to marriage).

Marriages are different; families are different; people are different. We are all in different stages of knowing ourselves, working on our healing, and being able to communicate well. But working towards trust and respect is a place we probably all need to be in. It sure does make the journey go more smoothly.

JODY

Marriage is under attack, and for good reason. The union between one man and one woman can change how we view love. If the couple is striving for holiness, as we know as Catholics, marriage is an outward sign of God's love, and the target to destroy it makes sense.

Since I was ten years old, I have wanted to be married. I wanted to *give* myself to someone fully and completely without fear. I found a man who I thought would do whatever it takes to have a successful marriage, persevere through the tough times. I chose wrong, and twenty-one years later, suffered the most horrific events in my life.

I didn't come from a good example of marriage, so I made inner vows at a young age that "I will never divorce, abandon, or give up." These vows made it difficult to make healthier decisions for myself when the time came. I thought since God was drawing me in closer to a deep relationship that he would take care of my marriage when things got bad (anxious attachment/quid pro quo/love with strings attached—all through the lens of my woundedness). But when he didn't, that's when our relationship ruptured.

I couldn't wrap my head around, "How could God allow this when he created it?" I was willing to do anything for what is good and beautiful, but was God on my side? The list of questions was endless. It wouldn't be until seven years later that my relationship with God would experience repair (which we are still working through).

I never left the Church or stopped having conversations with God. I was raw, real, and very angry. I let Jesus know every day how my heart hurt and how I questioned everything about him. My faith was tested!!! So, everything I said above I would have to put into action. Did I mean what I said and believed? This needed to play out.

Mother Church defines the purposes of marriage in an ambiguous way: to get your spouse to heaven and procreate. What the flip does that mean, and what does it take to do that? Marriage is a sacred vocation where it takes two people to commit their inner beings to each other. If both are not fully in, then there is no vocation.

So, what does it take to get your spouse to heaven? The only way is to fully engage in an intimate vulnerability with the Lord. One way to get there is by the individual taking responsibility to attend to their wounds. A good therapist will help you process each knot that has you captive and prevents you from loving more freely. Marriage will bring out the undercurrents of your attachment wounds from childhood. Our unhealthy attachments from childhood dictate how we will attach to God and our spouse. If you allow God to teach you how to have a *secure* attachment, that will open your heart to the deepest love. Growing with your spouse in search of that daily can only happen if you both are on the same team.

Blended families is another topic that would need its own

chapter. There is not much said in the Church about it and how to go about it in a healthy way. I am currently engaged to someone with children, and I find myself questioning everything. However, at the end of the day, if God has the confidence in me and I trust in his graces, we will work through the details as they happen.

Don't get me wrong. I have a lot of questions, and I'm aware of how fragile the situation is. Moreover, I have had to examine what this family dynamic is bringing out in me and tackle any insecurities, doubts, and fears with the Lord, my spiritual director, friends, and future spouse. Ask the Lord for the army you will need to face these tough emotions and thoughts. But for now, here are some suggestions that could help anyone, in any phase of life, pursue a healthy, holy, flourishing marriage they desire:

1. Pray together (examples: Lectio Divina, Rosary, from the heart, or structured prayer)
2. Make the home a place of worship
3. Prioritize what is rightly ordered: God, vocation, children, work, everything else
4. Work on your wounds: understanding your triggers, attachment style, and self-care (what fills your cup and makes you feel like *you*)
5. Self-sacrifice in a healthy way
6. Find individual spiritual directors
7. Practice the hierarchy of the home (husband, wife, children)
8. Seek out ways to protect your marriage from spiritual attacks

If any of this sounds new or you're unsure about the list, consult your priest or spiritual director or find conferences on these topics.

There is so much to be said. I pray for a holy, healthy, and joyful marriage for all of you and soon for me as well!! God bless, and let the adventure continue.

THE CONVERSATION CONTINUES

One of my mentors once said, "Your children are your ministry, and your spouse is your vocation." My current season of life with toddlers and babies has me pouring myself into their daily needs, education, and formation. However, one day, they will be grown up and out of the house. I need to be pouring myself into my marriage as well. Sometimes, it all seems exhausting. Christ wants me to welcome him into that exhaustion. He wants to help me be the wife and mother I am called to be. With him, "all things are possible," (Philippians 4:13).

Vicky T.

I can remember dreamily staring at Jerome after we had been dating a while, thinking, "There is nothing I would change about him." Yet, one of the qualities I liked best about him was that he was willing to change. He can't be stuck in his ways! That was so important to me.

If I learn something, Jerome is open to listening and usually making a change. So much has been turned upside down in our lives since we first got married. Eight kids, with eight unique personalities, gifts, and challenges, will do that. Our willingness to change has been pushed to the limit throughout our marriage as we reevaluated our diet, hobbies, time-management, parenting styles, discipline, spending habits, prayer life, and the list goes on.

The other side of the coin of change is: Where is it originating? Change must come from God. If not—we've all made bad decisions and know how that works out! Jerome and I prayed together before going to sleep for much of our marriage. We don't have a TV in our room, so every night we spend time talking. Before we're ready to go to sleep, one of us will say, "Well, do you want to say prayers?" These prayers aren't elaborate, and frankly, sometimes they don't quite make sense as one spouse struggles to stay awake. But these prayers reveal our hearts to each other and bring God into our relationship. Ultimately, it's the Holy Spirit who opens people to new ideas and change. A willingness to change, guided by the Holy Spirit, is such a gift in a marriage.

Angela W.

One-and-a-half years of marriage now: it's been great, adventurous and challenging. Not long ago, I said to my husband, "My love, I think our honeymoon phase is over."

In the beginning, everything seemed very easy and smooth. Now, we are at a point where we realize that we have to fight for each other—and we want to fight for each other. Also, the great thing is that marriage is a sacrament. We made the vow to always stay faithful to each other. Instead of running away from the difficulties, let's run into them, together with God and each other, and make it through, because we know that God gives us the grace to make it through. That gives us both so much safety, to know that we vowed to stay faithful, always, "Till death do we part!"

And then we've also found it's important to talk, talk, talk. In my experience, that is the most helpful. Talk openly to each other. Talk to a spiritual director. Talk to trusted friends. Talk to God. Don't be ashamed or scared to reach out to other friends/mentors to talk about your struggles because the struggles are real for everyone. But everything that is brought to the light can be healed!

Chiara D.

Five years into marriage, and the thing I have most learned about the sacrament is that it is so very different from how I dreamt it would be. As someone who spent the majority of their young adult life studying "Theology of the Body" and the Church's teachings on marriage, I walked into marriage arrogantly assuming I had already read the manual on how to have a holy and healthy marriage.

Boy, was I wrong. Was it incredibly beneficial for me to have rooted myself in those teachings before ever getting married? Absolutely. But I think what I have learned most about marriage in these first five years is that it is a *path* to holiness. It gives us daily opportunities to grow in holiness, if we choose to do so. It is the means for our purification—the process of removing our impurities—and therein, by no means pleasant.

Marriage demands us to look at our pride, stubbornness, selfishness, and so many other sins we didn't even know we had in us. It questions: *Do you want to hold onto these? Or do you want to honor your wedding vows more than your pride?*

When we said our vows, we took on the entirety of the other person, which includes all of the things we love about them but also all of the things we don't like about them.

Both the husband and wife bring to the table their own unique crosses and baggage. These things can all too often hinder our ability to see and love the other in the way they deserve to be loved, and it can also hinder our growth in holiness. But if we listen to Christ, we might just hear him say, "Pick up not only your cross but also your spouse's cross and follow me."

I believe *this* is where we discover the path to holiness that marriage provides - when we decide to love our spouse for God's sake. All this is not to excuse behaviors that harm the other—for Christ does not intend for each of us to be anything but loved—but this is to say that we are all works in progress and that a holy marriage is something we walk towards, not something any of us have fully attained.

Chanelle K.

I thought I understood the meaning of the words found in the Book of the prophet Jeremiah, "For I know the plans I have for you…" but then I would write things in my journal like "I will be married by the age of twenty-two or twenty-three at the latest." Looking back, I clearly missed the point of that verse!

I wanted to be a wife and mother, and I wanted it in my time, but his plan took much longer. In the 1980s, waiting past your early twenties to get married was not a thing! If you weren't married by twenty-four, it felt like something was dreadfully wrong. Each year that ticked past made my heart heavier and heavier, so, by the time I turned twenty-seven, I was beginning to feel like a forgotten old maid. I had lost sight of the fact that our God is a God of surprises.

As decades of a beautiful marriage have unfolded, I can say I am so grateful he made me wait! Marriage and all its many challenges and blessings are worth protecting, preserving, and cherishing—even when it's hard or the sacrifices seem a little out of balance. The truth is, love requires sacrifice . . . always!

I'd like to offer some advice to keep your marriage strong and to help you and your spouse feel loved and respected. Start with the bookends of your day. Begin each new day with the same question, "How can I pray for you today?" This simple question offers deep insight into the stress, worry, joy and challenge your spouse faces in the day ahead. End each day with a quick chat about the blessings and challenges of the day and share where you saw God in your day. Sometimes we get so caught up in "life," we don't notice all the ways God is loving, guiding, protecting, directing and correcting us until we think back and call it out with thanksgiving. The more we look for him, the more we will find him.

The job of each husband and wife is to help each other get to heaven, so be thankful for the many ways your spouse loves, supports, and encourages you. Be sure to mention the things you notice your spouse doing for you and your family. Be a prayer warrior for your spouse: use prayer to defend them in the struggles and celebrations they face, the ones you see and the ones that dwell in their heart. Every time my husband comes to mind during the day, I tell God, "Thank you for choosing him for me," and I follow that thought with a Hail Mary.

I waited a long time for God to show me the spouse he planned for me, and he is a treasure. Even when we don't see eye to eye or he's bugged the snot out of me for the umpteenth time, I remind myself that I'd be lost without him. I hold my words until I've given the Holy Spirit permission to craft them (most of the time). When I pray for the Holy Spirit's words, I'm very often aware that the problem lies in my stubborn pride.

We all await the rewards of heaven, where our only job will be to love and praise the Father. The sacrament of marriage gives us the grace to practice the deep and abiding love required for heaven every day with our spouse. Love and forgiveness are a stronger force than anything this world can throw at you, so beg God daily for the grace to love hard and forgive often.

Sheri W.

CHAPTER FOUR

Motherhood

Her children rise up and call her blessed;
her husband, too, praises her:

"Many are the women of proven worth,
but you have excelled them all."

PROVERBS 31:28–29

MARNEE

I keep thinking about how to start this chapter, and I really don't know which direction to go. How do I fit the motherhood experience in under 1500 words? Maybe how I waited so many years, working with so many wonderful kids—from my seven younger siblings to being a nanny in New York to working with orphans in Argentina—all the while just wanting to settle down, get married, and have ten kids of my own already!

Maybe how, when I did finally have a child, I was thirty-five years old, and my body, energy, and craving for kids had changed significantly since my teens and twenties. While so excited to be able to have a child, I think I felt every single day of pregnancy. The adjustment from being the master of my own body for three-and-a-half decades to turning it over completely to another human being was probably the most challenging transition I've had.

Then there is the part where having a child, living a life of totally self-sacrificial love (whether you want to or not sometimes!), is very healing of childhood wounds, totally mind-blowing as you watch your little one learn and grow, and such as source of deep joy, creating life-long treasures for you and your husband in your hearts.

In real time, as I write this, my little one is napping. That sounds pretty uneventful. Well, once you have children, you understand why everyone with children just can't seem to stop talking about all the little insignificant details at every available opportunity. Motherhood really takes over your life (and even something like napping can make your day)! That term, "takes over your life," often comes with a negative connotation, but I don't see it that way at all. What better endeavor to give your life over to than the raising and loving of a little person!

So, anyway, the nap situation is a saga, and while she has been resisting the needed two naps a day for the past week and has been cranky at predictable times as a result, the fact that she is now taking nap number two and we are leaving this evening to begin a trip is, in fact, a victory and such a relief! And it's also nice because it's during the nap times that I write—oh, she just woke up.

A-a-and, we're back. Eleven days later. After a week and a half of reflection, I still don't know how to sum up motherhood. I have seen some funny Instagram posts around Mother's Day recently, and I get the sense that no mom really knows how to explain what it's like to be a mom. "Hero" is one word that comes to mind. With all the awards and memorials out there, I really can't believe that there isn't one standing high above the rest that is for A MOM. There is a Catholic term that also comes to mind here: white martyrdom.

I have come to realize that the very best parts of life—those parts most loved, valued, enjoyed, and worth having—come with the intense self-sacrificing I am referencing above. So, in trying to sum up something like motherhood, do you talk about the challenges or the wonders? Does one cancel the other, or are they equal? It's simply not an equation or a simple reality. But . . . it is always worth it.

That is the one resounding thing I have heard from mothers. It's worth it.

I have a crayon drawing hanging up on our wall from a second grader I taught four years ago. It says "Yuor beautiful and worth it." I have kept it all these years because that phrase is ever true, and I need the constant reminder. (It also brings continual amusement, due to the misspelling.)

Every life is worth it. It just is. It's not because of some specific quality (i.e., it's easy, it makes us feel good, it gives us something, it's pleasant to behold). Life is just worth it. And being able to help create and/or raise a little life is worth it.

At this point, this discussion begins to cross over into other charged discussions in our culture today. And it's evident that without empirical proof or a certain percentage of positive experience (or anticipated experience), life can be considered "not worth it" for various reasons. This is a profound loss and a fundamentally difficult point to converse on.

But when you can reach the point of connection with the goodness of each human life, it will show through in all you say and do. Foster that. Whether through your chaotic life as mom, through your profound desire to be "Mom," or by whatever means you are given.

As Jennifer Fulwiler reiterates in her book *Your Blue Flame*, raising kids requires a village. Find your village, create your village, embrace your role and give it your all. Follow your gut, be in sync with your spouse, and spoil your little babies with love. They are worth it! And they are pretty darn adorable, too.

Let's also help each other end the mom shame and judgmental parenting. There are just *so* many ideas out there. Use your gut, your intuition. It's part of your mom superpowers. You can't spoil a baby. You don't have to turn into your parents. You may lose your patience or temper sometimes . . . just be real and human with your little blessing, apologize when needed, and your instincts will help you out a lot.

Now for the dark side of motherhood. Or at least the other side of the coin—the side that is less talked about, less understood, and has less written about it by the Church. The side where fertility is ultimately outside of our control. The side where your hearts and your home are ready and eager to welcome babies (or more babies), but they are not coming, or they are not staying.

In the course of writing this book, we had a miscarriage. At this moment, I am starting to take pregnancy tests, about two days away from knowing for sure if it's a positive or negative this cycle. (It turned out to be negative. And then the next two cycles were positive, followed by miscarriages.) We'd love to give a little sibling to our two-year-old. But after many tests and supplements and diet changes and some money, it just hasn't happened yet.

I was trying to explain to my husband a couple weeks ago the emotional roller coaster (or more like cliff jumping!) of entering into the fertility cycle each time. I couldn't really explain it because I don't really understand most of it myself. And each woman's fertility journey makes her own carnival ride of emotion a unique experience.

As women, we seem to be entrusted with the deepest emotional experiences. So profound on both sides of the spectrum that they cannot be explained, only felt. And we can share the knowledge of those feelings with other women.

These experiences do not make me wish away my womanhood. Instead, they show me what great depths I am uniquely capable of. And they carve out an inner world that is continually growing in intricacy that I could not have imagined. It resonates the mysterious biblical phrase "And Mary pondered all these things in her heart."

From a practical perspective, let's face it: unless someone has been on the journey, most people don't know what to say in the face of infertility or miscarriage. There are many wrong things said by well-meaning people. It's not what you want to hear or what you need to hear, and it's worse if it feels like the Church is saying it to you. But like so many things in life, we just don't know 'til we know. And even then, our experience of something could be different than another woman's.

We do know that loss is loss. And loss requires a certain amount of grieving and time and patience. We also know that loss comes in various guises. Is it the tangible loss of a baby in the womb? The loss of hopes and dreams and expectations? Maybe the loss of things happening in a specific way? Every time there is loss, it's best to let that person tell their story and not tell it for them. Yes, it may be uncomfortable for you, but not as difficult as it is for them...

Also, if people do say the wrong thing over and over again, I believe the best we can do is gently educate. There is never an excuse to respond with rudeness. Meanwhile, surround yourself with those who will take the time to listen or who can support you in a helpful way.

To all the mothers of heart and womb, your motherhood is essential, and you are essential. And to all those littles, you're lucky to have a mama who cares so much about your well-being and her own. #toughasamother

JODY

I don't know anything about birthin' no babies!!! This is a topic of which I am biologically ignorant. I suffered from infertility all my life, and now aging is against me. There is something that many in the Church refer to as being a "spiritual mother." After many years of suffering from infertility, I started to hear that phrase and hated it. It felt like a consolation prize, and I didn't need anyone's pity. Infertility challenged my femininity, my identity, and my purpose.

It was hard to wrap my brain around the fact that my body worked but was failing in some way. I was never able to find out the main cause, and that made my anger grow. This led me to lose hope in ever having biological children.

Then God does what he does and makes something beautiful happen. He allowed me to take care of women in crisis pregnancies and be the mother figure they needed. At the care center, I was free to love and care for them unconditionally and guide them through the toughest times in their lives. I was asked to be in the delivery room for three babies that would have been aborted. One child has my middle name. A small piece of me will always be with them, and I am forever blessed to have experienced that.

Back to infertility. No one can explain how devastating it is and how alone we feel. So, for those who haven't experienced infertility, please don't say the following: "Have you thought about adoption?" or "I'm sure if you pray more, it will happen," or "Have you been checked out?" Most likely, they not only have thought about those things, but they have also explored all options and are grieving.

Take this advice. If you know anyone suffering from infertility, remember that they are grieving. It's painful and *lonely*. Instead, ask them how you can best support them, or just hold space for them to express their experience. Don't make this about you.

It's uncomfortable for sure, and sitting with that is exactly what is needed. Silence is golden. They are not just grieving for not having a child; they are also grieving the future, their identity, where they fit in now, and motherhood. I understand you mean well. It's just important to know that infertility is complicated, deep, and a continuous suffering until the woman has gone through the grieving process. And there is no time limit on grief.

It wasn't until I turned forty-six years old that I dealt with it. I didn't realize the impact and the hole that was left. This suffering dictates your worthiness, how you live your life, and how you will love unless you face that loss and grieve it.

To all my infertile sisters. You are not alone in this! I've got you, and you don't have to be silent anymore. For many of us, we don't dare to talk about it because it's painful. You fear that you will bring everyone down or that you're being ungrateful, or you don't want to hear all the things you need to try or should be doing.

There are many infertility support groups, and therapy might be necessary. The best thing is to talk about it with your spouse. He needs to know, and probably you are both grieving.

Don't try to be the "strong" one. I did that, and it was the worst thing I could have done. I felt too embarrassed, ashamed, and like a failure. I wanted to stay hopeful and appear like it didn't bother me. I didn't want anyone to know that I cared about it. I didn't want to face the reality of the situation. It was too painful.

I felt an urgency to figure out what I was going to contribute to the world. What does infertility mean as a woman, and where do I fit in? I didn't allow others to console me in my loss. I hope you will find the courage to seek comfort in your pain and allow others to love you in the mess.

As Catholic women, we have implicit messaging about children—when to have them and how quickly after marriage to start. The pressure builds with every passing month, and the tension between you and your spouse begins to affect your relationship. We forget that we are not *entitled* to have children. They are products of marriage, a blessing, and a gift from God.

Sometimes, I've seen couples lose sight of what is rightly ordered. The vocation of marriage takes priority over the children. Some may have a difficult time adjusting to this concept. The family must be rightly ordered for the foundation to be rooted in God. God is first, then spouse, children, work, and everything else. I only wish I knew this twenty-five years ago. I hope this sparks some curiosity for you and that you seek counsel. It will change your relationship with God and your spouse. Ultimately, you will be free to flourish how God intended for *your* marriage and to bring light to the Kingdom.

Bless you all for your marriages, families, and devotion to God. Thanks be to God for saying YES to motherhood, no matter what form it takes.

THE CONVERSATION CONTINUES

"They will teach you what you need to know!"

This tidbit of wisdom was shared with me by an older mom, a stranger, in a passing moment of camaraderie. Twenty years later, it seems even wiser and more necessary.

During a quick naptime scroll, a young mom today might view a short video on gentle parenting techniques, another on nutrition, several funny posts about the impossibility of toddlers, and then a home makeover video showing her how to turn her daughter's room into a fairy-themed playground.

When her baby awakes forty-three minutes later, she will think ruefully of the series of reels she watched about sleep training, then feel a surge of guilt over the three nights in which she attempted this method, followed by a sense of failure over her baby's mutinously untrained schedule.

"They will teach you what you need to know" reminds us to put down the phone and trust in our ability to respond, with God's help, to our unique, incorrigible, delightful family's needs.

Of course, there may be times your baby tells you what you need to know, but you can't quite understand what they are saying. In such cases, feel free to consult your husband, a trusted older friend, a library book, or, if absolutely necessary, the internet.

When things are difficult, do research. When things go well, try to pay attention.

What I needed to know included breastfeeding for natural child spacing *and* healthy sleep habits for a happy child, but not which side was right in the baby sleep debates. It also included the specifications of dozens of dragons, how to create elaborate hair for Irish dance competitions, phonics for dyslexia, how to diagram a sentence, and what offside means in soccer. (Actually, I am still working on that last one.)

After twenty years, I still need them to teach me what I need to know.

Melinda O.

As a consecrated virgin, I find myself in such delight and awe, reveling in the mystery of Jesus calling me to be a "mother in the Spirit" to many people. I find it is a true gift to live the calling of "radical availability" to my Lover, Jesus, and to his children in the world who need the love and care of a sister, friend, or mother on the journey.

In the physicality of a woman's body, we understand our calling to love and become a gift of ourselves the more we contemplate this mystery. One way we see this is through God giving us wombs in which we can nurture and sustain life and welcome another person. This mission is for every woman, married or unmarried, religious or consecrated. We are to become a good home for people to be nurtured in life. A favorite quote of mine from Alice von Hildebrand speaking to women is, "You must create a nest of love, a place where it is good to be."

As a consecrated virgin, I love having my own home, a home in which I can welcome so many people in hospitality. Some people come who need a listening ear and a cup of tea, some need a place to stay for a night, some need a cocktail and dinner with me as a friend, and some want rest with the Lord and prayer. The important part is that Jesus has helped me cultivate a home where friends find the peace of Christ, welcome, and a good place to be.

Dawn H.

I remember learning about spiritual maternity when I first entered the convent. I was eighteen years old at the time, which means that everyone I worked with, unless they were kids, were either my age or older than me. How could I possibly be their mother? As the years passed, I grew into my spiritual maternity. After the birth of my first nephew, I wrote a long reflection to my sister-in-law about being mothers!

As a Spouse of Christ, I really bring forth his children. I can't say that I have accompanied many people to be reborn in Christ through baptism, but after baptism, the image of Christ in each person must be nurtured into perfection. That's what I do. I love and pray and accompany people into their full potential as children of God. I can always be sure to receive a Mother's Day greeting from my sister-in-law. God is good!

Sr. Holy Family

After two years of marriage, we discerned that it was time to apply as foster parents, since we passed Ennis Center for Children every day on the way to work. Looking back, the process seemed so easy: in January, we inquired, in February, we started our classes, and by May, we had our license to begin foster parenting. On June 8th, Victoria was born, and she has been with us ever since! Seeing and hearing about other foster family stories, however, made us realize that Victoria's birth into our family was truly a miracle, and we probably shouldn't count on that a second time. We did keep our foster license active, though, "just in case."

Victoria taught me how to love someone else with a selfless love I never knew was inside of me. The first thirty years of my life were all about me . . . and it's been a very gradual change since . . . which illustrates another quality of God: His patience! She also was born with a laugh that came out at one month old! She would sit on the couch with Shannon in the evenings and laugh with a deep belly roar that I never heard from someone so tiny . . . another sign that God himself must be All Funny, since he himself created this little angelic being.

When Victoria was two years old, I read a book on homeschooling and was intrigued by this beautiful picture of parenting that homeschooling seemed to provide. This is what convinced me to start the application with Adoption Associates in order for Victoria to have a younger sibling. "You can't just homeschool one child," I naively thought.

Hannah was born the following March, twelve weeks before her due date, weighing just over two pounds. Both my mom and Shannon knew the great importance of simply holding a baby, so the three of us would take turns driving down to Henry Ford Hospital in Detroit in order to hold Hannah. (Thank you, Mom!!)

After almost two months, much of which was spent in an incubator (and a growth of three more pounds), Hannah entered our family on Mother's Day in 2007. It was amazing to watch her tiny body grow and her desire to learn right along with it.

Despite the outlook at the beginning of her delicate life, Hannah grew to be the best student in our family and a girl who loves to read all kinds of books, who enjoys playing most sports, and someone who knows all the tricks of outdoor survival and camping. She especially has a big heart for her younger siblings and young ones in general, considering even a future in teaching. Thank you, God, for Hannah!

Since we had our foster license still active, we received a phone call from our friends at Ennis only a month after bringing Hannah home: Victoria had a little brother who needed a home immediately. Soon after that phone call, sure that Victoria especially would be so blessed to grow up with her own biological sibling, we brought home this cute six-month-old baby boy!

For a whole week, we enjoyed Chase's wonder with the world around him. Then he discovered the art of crawling . . . and by eight months old, Chase was walking. My dear mom sincerely asked how she could be of help the day we brought Chase home. "Mom, please just pray that Chase sleeps the night."

He slept ten straight hours that first night and every night thereafter. Hannah was the perfect complement of a sister to Chase: though she often needed to feed during the night in order to continue gaining strength, she had an inner sleep schedule during the day that she kept even past two years old. Hannah and Chase grew up as "Irish twins" and became close friends along the way.

So, being a mom to Hannah and Chase and Victoria was completely "it" for me as a mom . . . no need to search any further. I was finding joy and peace in being their mom, and they were teaching me so much, too!

After a year, however, we received another phone call (since we had decided to keep our foster license active, "just in case"). There were two children, Brittany (four years old) and Salvadore (two years old), who needed a home for a short-term basis only.

Their mom was a recent immigrant from Mexico and wasn't quite aware of social etiquette in this country. She had left her two young children unattended in their apartment for the few minutes it took for her to go down to her car and back upstairs. Instead of having sympathetic neighbors (as she assumed they would be), one of them called CPS.

The social worker called us a bit frantic because they were "unable to find Spanish speaking foster parents in either Wayne or Oakland counties." She mentioned, apologetically, that she was aware of our current household with three young ones already, but they really needed help.

If the current me was put in this same situation sixteen years ago and asked that same question, I would've said, "No, sorry, Ms. Karen; can't do it and won't." But grace works in our naivety sometimes, as it did then for us.

"Yes, for sure. No problem! We're available." Soon after, we were taking care of five children four years old and younger.

It was during those two months that I learned how scheduling was a big help when necessary. We followed a tight schedule for meals, bedtime, playtime, etc., and the days went by smoothly and quickly. It was after Brittany and Salvador were reunited with their beautiful mom that I appreciated all the more my own three young children and the lack of a tight schedule . . . being more spontaneous felt like a better fit, personally.

Soon after that brief period, we found out some other news: I was expecting Dominic! From the moment I found out, through the next nine months, through delivery, and beyond, I couldn't stop laughing. Every conversation caused me to burst out laughing. "God is so funny!"

This is the phrase I used most every day when sharing the news of our "unplanned pregnancy." We had spent time and money in the past with this goal in mind (always working with Catholic doctors and trying to follow their advice), but now we were a happy, fully content family with no desire to ask for more gifts . . . and now God decided that this was a great time for Dominic to enter the world! He was conceived during that very busy time, and all I could do from then on was contemplate God's immense sense of humor!

My kids saved me from a life of selfishness and self-centeredness!

The gift of knowing God's great love for us is different from actually putting it into practice . . . to where you are willing to accept heart-hurts and pains for your loved ones.

Being a mom opened me up to this love in action, for which I am *so* grateful. There are so many beautiful, consecrated souls who achieve great heights of love in practice, but I think God knew that my thick head and heart needed to see precious, dependent, innocent little ones in my daily life. Isn't it amazing that God entrusts these innocent little ones to often immature adults, waiting patiently for us to grow up and learn what is really important?

Growing up, my heroes did not include stay-at-home moms. Mother Teresa was a hero for sure (especially her missionary sisters in Africa, for some reason!), but also any finisher of the Ironman triathlon or any woman in the Air Force. Being a mom did not fit in my plans for life, until later, after "living" a bit. I look back and can see how God gently took my selfish being and allowed me to live with happy/holy ladies for a few years until he was finally able to communicate clearly his great love.

I admire *so* much the young parents who are ready for a life of sacrifice at the young age of twenty-twoish. God bless them!!!

Katherine W.

CHAPTER FIVE

Vocational Discernment

She picks out a field and acquires it;
from her earnings she plants a vineyard.

PROVERBS 31:16

MARNEE

Vocational discernment is a beautiful and sometimes painful journey of exploring our deepest desires *between us and God*. That definition probably didn't get fully ironed out for me until I was thirty-three years old, unexpectedly meeting my husband.

When I think of vocational discernment, unfortunately, the first image that comes to mind is a Mother Superior telling me that by going off to do mission work in Argentina and not joining her order, I was running away from God's will for me. Yikes!

That was definitely not the first or last time I would be told by an authority figure what my vocation was and judged for feeling impelled to follow a different path. I know this is the story of so many others as well.

Fortunately, there are also those figures of wisdom and experience (and many with invaluable common sense) that speak truth into our lives. One such person was a priest friend with a charism for discernment retreats who helped both my husband and me (individually, before we met) to identify and follow our true callings. It may take some time to really tune our ear to it, but at a certain point along our journey, we know Truth when we hear it. Whether we want to hear it or not, it has a presence that is undeniable.

It is a very intimate thing to be open to the desires of your heart. And it can cause a lot of pain if you are aware of them, but they are not fulfilled year after year. I can't explain why this is the case for so many—myself included—but I do know it is not worth it to settle for less just for the sake of impatience or pain. Sometimes, it feels like an odd test of endurance to see if we can last virtuously until our vocation can be realized.

Yes, of course, we strive to live the waiting part well, and it's very helpful to our vocation when we do, but that deep longing is simply not quenched until we reach it. I think that angst and unmet desire propel us forward and keep us from compromising if we can allow ourselves to live with its intensity.

God is a God who loves you and loves how he made you. You don't have to check certain boxes for perfection or lead a life others describe as the right one for you. God may speak through others to help you realize your calling, but keep that ear out for Truth. It brings peace, strength, clarity, hope. It does not bring judgment, pressure, or sweep you into a general category based on your external actions.

For those of us who have had a lot of intellectual formation in the Church, we can get a little heady when it comes to discernment. We know St. Ignatius's discernment of spirits, St. Teresa's way of perfection, St. Therese's little way, St. Francis' renunciation of worldly goods, etc. We also know the litanies and rosaries and novenas that help with making decisions and that promise swift results.

We can overthink what would be the most pleasing decision to God that we could make or the best possible path for our lives. And what happens when we've prayed the St. Anne novena for our future husband for the third year in a row leading up to her feast day, and we've just had one relationship after another, end with no husband in sight?

It can be really counter-cultural (even in the Church) to pursue the bold and beautiful desires of your heart, to go with your feelings in the sense of those really deep feelings that act like a signpost towards the unique and essential path to which God calls you. I can't remember where I heard it, but there is a quote attributed to Mother Angelica that I use as a sort of motto: "If you want God to do the miraculous, you must be willing to do the ridiculous." I'm sure her dream of Catholic television sounded ridiculous to many along the way!

If you think about it, you being the wildly unique person God made you to be is exactly what all the evil forces want to keep you from. In fact, it may also be what your own woundedness tries to tell you that you're not good enough for. All the more reason to rise up in battle for yourself and your happiness!

Remember, God is never the one telling you that you are not good enough for the calling he gave you. That is contradictory and wouldn't make sense. If there is resistance, it comes from elsewhere and likely bears the feelings of shame, pride, fear, or confusion.

A note for the well-formed who are living the Christian life. We aren't likely to fall for major sins and temptations that would obviously derail us. We're going to fall for the lofty intellectual arguments that lead to self-doubt and confusion. Or the scrupulosity that makes us think we are damned, short of perfect performance (not to mention the contradicting ideas about how to reach absolute perfection!). Or maybe we'll hang on every word of a spiritual authority we have raised on a pedestal and who might like the sound of their own voice too much.

We, the thoroughly catechized, can get caught up in complex arguments and comparisons and virtue talk to the point of being stagnated in our discernment. At that point, even going to God is confusing, and we believe he is just as frustrated with our struggle as we are.

Let's break free and be radical and follow God with the openness and unpredictability of the Holy Spirit, who "blows wherever he wills." Let's believe God is gentle, loving, and knows that we are struggling even before we do. Let's also believe that

God can handle our stumbling, and we are not big enough to inadvertently mess up his plans while we try to wrestle through all the thoughts and voices coming our way.

Take heart! Your intentions have been in the right place all along. You just need to get comfortable with a little messiness in life, as Pope Francis likes to remind us.

My vocational journey has taken zigs and zags, but the heart of it has always been towards marriage. Even when it got into my head for a time that it was the less perfect and more earthly path, I just couldn't shake the calling for long. Sometimes, my possible calling to the religious life was explored more vigorously after an especially hard breakup or in moments of despair that marriage couldn't intrinsically be a good experience. Or maybe when I was so tired of having to make so many life decisions while feeling like I was groping around in the dark, I just wanted to have a superior tell me what to do.

Overall, my view of the two major vocational paths has been like comparing silver and gold. Both are precious and beautiful and good, but one always shining more brightly for me than the other. I have heard many difficult stories of those who chose religious life or marriage out of a place of brokenness, and the resulting experiences caused so much pain. Then there are stories that are deeply mysterious, where it almost seemed like God called a person to one for a time, then to the other.

However it looks for you, it's okay to keep the quiet inner workings to yourself if you don't find you're in a godly, supportive community. It all comes down to you and God anyway, no matter what vocation you enter into.

JODY

Hmmm. What to say about this? I didn't have my faith growing up, so I didn't know about discerning your vocation. At the age of ten, I knew I wanted to be a wife. Not until recently did I consider discerning a vocation. However, I told God that there is no way religious life is an option for me, haha.

Being a woman in her forties discerning religious life is very hard. I had already been married, and my heart still ached for it. The Lord and I hashed it out for a few years about what was next for us until he introduced me to third orders for lay members.

In late 2023, I started to research and pray about where he might want me. All I knew at that point was that I could have the religious community and marriage. Why not? The best of both worlds! So, I dove right in, and the Lord led me to the Third Order Dominicans.

I am in my first year as an inquiry. The discernment takes a total of five years. So, it will take some time for it all to play out. I am excited about it and enjoying the process.

Just a side note: every third order has different requirements and processes.

I can only speak to what I learned about single life and how that was my "vocation" for the past nine years until this past May. There is much debate about singlehood being a vocation. In my opinion, it is not.

It has been the hardest way to live out the faith. You don't have any real direction that a "formal" vocation offers. You are either a religious, married, or consecrated in some way (deacon, consecrated virgin, etc.).

I had a friend suggest to me that I live out my baptismal

vows and make my baptism the focus and direction that I need to serve others, pursue the Lord, and mature in my faith. I was lost, confused, and frustrated in what felt like "limbo." So, it was difficult to accept. What does my current state in life mean as far as a vocation?

Single life is a time for getting to know yourself, the Lord, and purifying your heart. During this time, I have experienced great healing, understanding, and have grown in a more mature love for God. Discerning what God wants for your vocation is in the daily suffering of being alone. However, you can have a lot of the same struggles in marriage or in religious life.

If that's the case, what does it mean to discern your vocation? First, the possibility that you are exactly where you need to be. Second, examine if you truly believe God has your ultimate good in mind in the situation you are in. You may believe he does, but somehow you may not feel it. If that is the case, that could be coming from a wound or how your attachment to God is playing out. This would need more exploration, which, if you are single, you have the time to do.

Third, stop praying it away if God isn't removing it yet. Instead, ask the Lord for the graces to help you endure this situation. By doing this, you are increasing your love and trust in the Lord. Of course, it's okay to ask the Lord to take you out of the situation or fix it, but if he's still permitting it, then give him the authority in your situation and lean into the suck. You will be surprised at what you find there.

Most of what we are feeling during this time is the discomfort of being out of control or the fear of the unknown. We ought to enter into that space, invite the Lord into that suffering, and endure the feelings. We are trying to avoid the feelings that this situation brings. Again, look at your attachment to the Lord. He wants to create a secure attachment to you by allowing you to feel the suffering, process what is coming up for you (possible wound), and waiting for you to invite him to comfort you.

My hope is that we can all learn to discern with the confidence that God has our greater good in mind. He will lead us to the vocation that he had planned when we were created, and he will give you a fulfilling life with him. "Stop, drop, and pray" is the way to God's heart.

THE CONVERSATION CONTINUES

"Oh, she's definitely going to be a nun."

As a young, single woman, I had often heard the older ladies at church whisper about me in this way. I thought, "Well, God, if that's what you want for me, why are you telling them and not me?"

It seemed that everyone was certain that because of my love for the Lord, it was the only appropriate course of action for me to leave my family and join a convent. The implicit danger here, however, was that this kind of thinking created a dichotomy where I could not desire marriage and desire holiness at the same time.

Fed up with everyone else "knowing" that I was meant to be a nun, one year for my Lenten promise, I told God that I would discern my vocation every day. I made a resolution that by the end of the forty days, I would know his will for me. I got to day twenty, where I sat before the Blessed Sacrament, and God so gently reminded me, "My timeline, not yours, love." I was so lovingly humbled!

I heard in a talk once on vocations that to discern is also a call, that discernment in itself bears witness to others. As I write this, I am still single, still not a member of any convent, and still contemplating consecrated singlehood. I spent all of my twenties asking God why he hadn't called me yet, but in my thirties, I am reminded that not being in any of the three main vocations does not mean that God has forgotten about me or that I do not have a calling or that my life has not started yet.

Though frustrating to be in a state of waiting and searching, the season of vocational discernment is where God prepares us and nurtures us. I would love to know by tomorrow where God is calling me, but I am also so very happy for this season to be just me and God.

Angie E.

I think, for me, the most important part of vocational discernment is the private relationship I have with Christ. I could spend my whole life dreaming about what I would like to do or what fits with my talents, interests, gifts, etc.

Vocation means call. It's his call. He doesn't get it wrong. As the one who created all my gifts, talents, and capacities, he knows all the undiscovered ones, too! I believe God leads us by giving us good desires. That's why one of the confirmations I have that I am "in my vocation" is that my life is everything I ever wanted (and more). That's not without its ups and downs, its crowns and crosses. Through it all, my vocation as consecrated to him is my underlying foundation of love and that from which I draw my energy.

Sr. Holy Family

When I was young, I wanted to be a nun—well, honestly, I was too young to really know anything except what people around me told me: that, effectively, since I liked church, I should be a nun. Makes sense, right? Well—not really!

As I came into high school, I began dating and desiring a relationship. However, what had been repeated in my ears rang in my head loudly—maybe I was going to end up as a religious sister regardless of what I thought I wanted.

Fast forward to college. I continued to date but always in the back of my mind, I figured I could still be "open" to religious life. The clincher? I didn't even slightly desire religious life.

I had gone on vocational discernment retreats, terrified that God would "call me" to religious life ("terrified" being the key word). I believe I kept going out of a sense of obligation to truly give this beautiful life a chance. However, the practice was consistently rooted in anxiety and dread.

When I finally sat down with a spiritual director quite a bit later in college, he simplified it for me. He looked me in the eye and said, "Raechel, do you want to be a nun?"

I surprised myself by saying, "No."

He replied, "Then don't be!"

I was shocked. Was it that simple? But it was and is. We will fall in love in one way or another. Sometimes, falling in love means falling into the beautiful world of religious life (or profound service in the single life), and sometimes, it means falling into the arms of the man you want to build a life with. Either way, I always try to remember that vocation is all about how we serve God—how we can best pave the way to heaven for those placed in our care and our lives.

No path is easy, but the goal is the same. Most importantly, we need to remember that where we complicate, God clarifies, and when we land in chaos, God is the peace. Follow the peace!

Raechel W.

I mentioned that my motives for deciding on entering the consecrated life were not purely out of love for God, though I felt the calling to a life dedicated to him even as a little girl. Yet it was there that I learned the incredible beauty and depth of our Catholic faith *and* his true presence in the Holy Eucharist!

The pace of life was very fast—some people were able to live it and keep healthy physically (five minutes of free time twice a day, for example, was enough for one of my friends to learn a foreign language!), but it took its gradual toll on my health.

After three-and-a-half years, I was almost fifty pounds less than when I entered (and my cycle had stopped at the beginning of this time period).

Though physically I wasn't flourishing, this was a profoundly special time of seeing such beauty in the lives of consecrated souls in love with the person of Jesus. I look back at that gift of time spent there as a piece of heaven . . . our days centered around the Holy Eucharist and charity was the air we breathed! Not once do I remember any bad word spoken of anyone by anyone, truly a miracle of God's grace given that we were more or less a hundred ladies living together in the formation period!!

At the same time, though, living in that consecrated world was like trying to put on a glove that just wouldn't fit. So, when my superiors told me the news that my body weight was at the point of worrying them enough to send me home, a huge figurative weight was lifted! This was a special moment of learning God's personal and deep and intimate love for *me*! He cares about *me* and wants *me* to be happy! Yes, he's quite consoled when we offer our prayers and sacrifices and live in reparation for sins and for the salvation of souls! But at the same time, *he loves us* and wants us *happy*!

During this awesome formation period, I was able to learn through some wonderful classes that happiness isn't found in doing whatever feels good at the moment. He had given me that period to learn and understand my faith and the meaning of "freedom" (a concept I had a hard time understanding the first year especially).

So, I was given the blessing of going home under God's goodness, the promise of obedience I had made, the intellectual formation, and the great, great love he showered me with on that day of departure. As a result, I came home full of life—full of love for God and love for this life he had given me! Next year will mark thirty years since I left the consecrated life, yet those three and a half years were a solid base I was allowed to receive in preparation for what life would one day bring me.

Katherine W.

Upon finishing high school and entering college, God did not allow me to remain at peace with my then "lukewarm" faith. He wanted the front burner of my life, and he invited me into a deeper relationship with him. The way I had been living was not satisfying me anymore.

So, I began seeking God. I questioned many things about my Catholic faith because of friends who asked me about saints, Mary, the Eucharist, and many other beliefs we hold true. I thank them today for helping me take my faith and God more seriously.

I began getting involved in the local student parish, attending retreats, going to daily Mass, reading Scripture, and finding friends in the Catholic faith. There was a point when a friend of mine asked me, "Dawn, have you discerned your vocation?" I really hadn't thought about it and just assumed I was getting married one day. However, when I dated guys, deep down, I knew that something was just not right. I had a "restless heart," and I was unable to move forward with relationships.

My friend continued, "You know that any good Catholic would ask *God* what he wants you to be, what *his* calling is for you." At that moment, my friend's words planted a seed of discernment in my heart. Around that same time, I met a consecrated virgin for the first time while going to daily Mass at a local parish. My curiosity grew to want to know more about the consecrated life in general.

While on mission, I told God, "Okay, God, you have one year to call me to a religious order. I can't date while on mission, so here is your opportunity." I realized that when we give God just a bit of room to lead our lives, he so graciously receives it and does beautiful things with it.

He was ever so gently working on my heart that year. I was in contact with religious sisters and ended up living with them in their convents. Yet, my heart was still restlessly searching for something different for me. I also remembered feeling so alive in faith and intimacy with Jesus whenever I found myself alone in the sisters' chapel or out on a walk by myself. The common denominator was when I was by myself with the Lord.

Upon returning from mission, I met a wonderful woman who was a consecrated virgin who became my mentor and friend. I found myself drawn to her and desiring to understand more of the mystery of her life as a bride of Christ. She looked like the rest of us, dressed in beautiful feminine modesty, yet she was very different. She radiated a joy that was not of this world, the joy of belonging to her Beloved, Jesus, while living in the midst of the world and working as a youth minister.

She spoke of her life with Jesus just as someone would speak of the love of a spouse on earth. She talked about date nights with *God* and of the freedom and joy she had living forever committed to God alone, espoused to her Maker! She was filled with zeal to do whatever her Spouse asked of her, to go wherever he led her to serve, to love and to pray for his people. I could tell that she was a woman in love—in love with God! The love they shared overflowed to great fruitfulness and generosity to share that love with the world.

In my skepticism, I thought, "Is it really possible for someone to experience being in love with God as if with a man on earth?"

The more I spent time with her, the more I trusted this to be true. My attraction to the beauty of marriage with a man on earth began to be transformed to a deeper yearning for the marriage of heaven—marriage with Jesus alone, the only Man that could truly fulfill this heart of mine.

Discerning a call to consecrated virginity was not a smooth journey. I experienced a rollercoaster of emotions daily from fears of what this journey would mean for me, fears of what it would cost me, yet I also experienced the most radical joy, peace, and life in this path, which was new to my heart.

I had a deep yearning to spend time with God alone more and more and a desire to help others learn to know and love God, too. Recognizing this call in myself was as if I just met myself for the first time! I realized who I was meant to be and what I was designed for!

It brought a great sense of joy and desire to love God more deeply and serve God's people with new passion and grace. My heart was finally able to rest in the trust and peace that only God can bring when you are on the right path. I never felt more alive until I was discerning the call to belong to Christ alone, espoused to him forever, being a living witness to the world of our ultimate destiny: intimate union with God!

In November of 2019, I was given the greatest gift of my life as I walked down the cathedral's aisle in a wedding dress to be wedded to our Lord Jesus through the hands of my bishop. I thank the Lord for this great gift—being a bride of Christ not only in this life but into eternity! Thank you, Jesus!

Christian discernment of life's choices and of one's vocation should be experienced as an exciting and holy adventure with our God, one that grows intimacy with and trust in our Lord and his divine providence for our lives. Sometimes there is much waiting and longing involved . . . awaiting answers and gifts from him. With these moments, do not despair or get disheartened. Keep awaiting the Lord in expectant faith and joyful hope.

Other times, there is great joy and peace when discovering the glory of plans unfolding before our eyes of his will for us. "Find your delight in the Lord / who will give you your heart's desire. / Commit your way to the Lord; / trust in him and he will act . . ." (Psalm 37:4–5).

In discernment, we must be careful of any desperate or anxious grasping for ourselves, which is a tendency since the Fall. We must learn to vulnerably wait upon the Lord and act when he prompts us to move forward in some way towards the vocation to which he is calling us.

When we encounter the state in life vocation that God is calling us to, we should experience a sense of God's peace, joy, clarity, and an "at-homeness" where we are most fully alive and ourselves. Our vocation is a calling to love someone—a man on earth or God directly—and sometimes it takes encountering the right person, religious community, or another form of consecrated life to awaken that calling.

Dawn H.

CHAPTER SIX

Work and Service

She puts her hands to the distaff,
and her fingers ply the spindle.

She reaches out her hands to the poor,
and extends her arms to the needy . . .

Acclaim her for the work of her hands,
and let her deeds praise her at the city gates.

PROVERBS 31:19–20, 31

MARNEE

*H*ow do we navigate the role of work and service in our female lives today? I keep asking myself that, and there just isn't a clear answer. It is very individual to each of us—our age, our state in life, the callings God puts in our hearts, our own level of honest self-awareness, the needs of those who are a part of our primary vocational state . . .

The subject of work among wives and mothers today is like two seas with different tides merging at a point. What I am sure you've encountered as well is that when the conversation of work comes up in these contexts, there are polarized experiences and opinions on how it should be approached. 1) Work as a wife and mom is encouraged, considered self-empowering—you do you. 2) Work as a wife and mom is discouraged, judged, and shame on you if you don't stay home full time with your children.

In fact, even if the topic is brought up online with a disclaimer that the poster is not looking for an argument, the haters or judgers just can't resist. (Gosh, what is it about the ability to post online that removes almost everyone's filters?)

So, clearly, this is a deeply emotional topic filled with struggle, shame, guilt, and triggers galore. Why? And is there a right answer? There can't possibly be one right answer when the variety of situations for wives and mothers out there are literally innumerable. However, maybe certain helpful questions can lead us to know our own hearts and give us peace and clarity in our decisions.

First of all, we are multi-talented women. Some of us have had degrees, careers, hobbies, side hustles, and various other areas of excellence before becoming wives or moms. Maybe we've had mixed feelings about it. Maybe we never wanted to pursue those things, but life mandated it. Maybe we are still waiting for marriage and struggle with what to pursue. Maybe we love what we have done and pursued but feel guilty about it for some reason.

God calls us to all sorts of things along our life journeys! Answering those callings can be a way to help you become fully yourself. But of course, the question is about the balance of these things in our life, whether we are married, waiting to be married, or will never be married.

I always think we best start by giving ourselves time and space for an honest heart examination of why we are considering engaging in a particular activity. Where is the draw coming from? God's calm and loving voice? The practical need to pay bills? The emotional and mental urgency of a woman who is floundering in her current situation? A deep wound of fear, insecurity, or struggle with identity?

Include the people who are significant in your vocation in your soul-searching. God won't be calling you to something that detracts from those people or that vocation. It can help bring clarity. How does your call resonate with them?

I do believe that when we are truly honest with ourselves and we identify callings, they are going to serve our whole vocation. Therefore, if each person is honest and discerning (though it may take time to get there), your calling will not only fill you with light and joy and excitement, but the rest of your household as well. It may just take a lot of communication, prayer, and humility to find that sweet spot of God's calling.

Since I am not a man, I really can't delve very deeply into the subject of men as sole or primary providers for their families. I keep telling my husband he needs to write a book for men about his own experiences and conversations with other men.

He says, "There is just something about men being able to

provide for their families." We haven't totally figured out what it is, but something is in there with a connection to provision, work, stability—something. Hopefully, we can take that as an encouragement to have open, non-shaming conversations with our husbands about the topic.

Sadly, I have seen men's desire to provide shut down by their wives. Perhaps this is because some women feel that a husband providing is somehow synonymous with control, power, or limits on her freedom. Well, it's not synonymous. If this theme brings our fears to the surface with a confusing intensity, that is for us to work through. On the other hand, if our husband is using his provision as a source of control and subjugation, that is something he needs to work through, and fast!

Most likely, at some point in this journey, God is going to call on you for profound trust. Like, maybe the "I feel like I am about to walk off the edge of a cliff, and I hope God is going to catch me (us)" type of trust. That's not a bad thing, but we are wired these days to be terrified of things we can't control.

When he does catch you on the other side, you'll be living a better life than before. Though it can get exhausting if this is asked of you over and over again, the reprieve will finally come . . . but I don't know when. Just know that through all those jumps, you've likely built a deeper faith than most that will serve you well.

We women have such a deep desire to give. We want to take care of our friends, be attentive to our neighbors, be connected to our siblings, be supportive to our parents, dote on our grandparents, be selfless for our kids, and be a total gift to our spouses. The reality is that living life to the best of our ability asks that from us naturally. We don't have to go looking for it! You don't *need* to add more to your plate.

You have nothing to prove to anyone.

You are already enough.

God will put in your life those he wants you to care for. He will bring your way the opportunities he wants you to be involved in. They will demand your all, in one way or another. If a true calling for something new comes along, follow it! But you can see where the need for careful discernment comes in.

We may follow a perceived call in order to be more loved, to be more perfect, to be more like other people, to fill a need for security or self-sufficiency, to distract ourselves from underlying pain, to chase after vanity, etc. The intense identity shift to motherhood (or even to marriage) can be one such cause for grasping at an external definition of productivity or a feeling of control.

It is a wonderful and powerful thing when a woman comes into her own and lives in the grace, beauty, and strength of her primary and secondary callings. If you encounter a woman living in this radiance with her husband, children, friends, family, or community sharing in her glow, affirm her and thank God for the grace he has given that has been received! Don't try to fit her into a specific mold that you yourself struggle with. Try not to be envious or find ways to pick apart her life. Yes, it is imperfect. That will always be the case.

If you encounter a woman struggling, heavy with shame, guilt, confusion, defensiveness, judgment, or anxiety, listen to her. Support her. Recognize her good intentions that have gotten buried under a difficult life, too many stressors, internal or external pressures, or years of opinions. Walk with her towards the light of where she is being led, not down the path that you may have uniquely found for yourself. It does no good to impose our unique path on another. If you have come into your own, you know better than most that God crafted each of those steps just for you, and you want him to do the same for every other woman, too!

JODY

Wow, this topic is tricky. Marnee said it well and expressed the dichotomy in which we, as women, find ourselves. I think work and service depend on what state of life you are in and what God is inviting you into. For me, I have worked since I was twelve years old. I never had the option to stay at home since I didn't have children. It was expected that I work. Work has always been a necessity and not a choice for me.

It seems that if you don't have children, you don't have the right to desire to stay at home. People laugh when you suggest being a stay-at-home wife. Why is that when our creation is to nurture the home, care for your husband, and raise the children? Just because God doesn't permit some women to have children, does that automatically forfeit the natural inclination to nurture? Why, as women, are we so hard on each other around this topic? I hope we can start looking at each other through the lens of empathy for the sake of loving our sisters and ourselves.

I can only speak on how God used work and service to lead me to a deeper relationship with him. "How?" you may ask - By showing me what brings out my gifts, the good that lies within, and what my limits were.

In nursing, God showed me the parts of myself that are nurturing, compassionate, empathic, comforting, and able to respond quickly. At the pregnancy care center, he showed me how I thrive when doing public speaking, expressing my passion for justice, and managing different roles. As a therapist, I used everything mentioned above as well as the ability to see patterns, listen, and wait for the Holy Spirit to speak. Of course, I also learned a drawback of my passion to serve others, which drives me to give the answers instead of allowing the time for the process to happen.

All of this to say, your work and service for others will allow you to flourish in your femininity in ways you never expected. Finding the balance is tough and deserves self-compassion during the process of ironing it out. Remember to seek God first in all you do, and he will provide the answer.

So, if you have to work because of your circumstances, take that opportunity to discover who you are during this time. You can ask yourself, What virtues can I practice? How do I feel towards this occupation? (i.e., What is the relationship I have with this job?) Does this job provide me the space to share the gift/talents God gave me? Are the demands of this position giving me time for self-care? Is this where God needs me, or is this just comfortable?

The point here is to reflect on how you can show the glory of God in work or service. Whatever work or service you find yourself in, you're beautifully created to fulfill God's plan. Your unique qualities as a woman are needed despite your insecurities. "I live, no longer I, but Christ lives in me; insofar as I now live in the flesh, I live by faith in the Son of God who has loved me and given himself up for me" (Galatians 2:20).

My sister in Christ, be free to be feminine in all you do. You will deprive us all if you don't.

THE CONVERSATION CONTINUES

Serving and loving my family has become the way I serve and love the Lord. The two are not separated in my mind but flow from one and the same love. Our vocation is that which allows us to best love, and what better way to serve the Lord than to love him in those he sent me? When I bathe, feed, and dress my children, these acts "done unto [Christ]" bring order to our home.

Our family strives to do acts of service during the penitential seasons of Advent and Lent that put our children in contact with the poor. Visiting nursing homes, making bagged lunches for shelters, and making meals for families in need are activities that are accessible for my young children. Not only do these activities bring us together but also offer an opportunity to grow in virtue. It's sometimes difficult to not get the cookies we just baked or watch all the snacks go in bags for the homeless. I tell my children that growing in virtue is meant to strengthen us. I have seen the fruit of their generosity and am floored by my children.

Cassie D.

What a tough topic for us women, many of whom are also mothers. Over the course of my life, the opinions of society have flip-flopped so many times regarding women at home. Is it healthy or holy to work outside the home? Is it good to serve outside of the home when there are still children at home to raise? The answer to both of these questions can be yes; alternatively, they can also be no. The key is finding the balance.

Finding the balance doesn't mean, "When everything is perfect at home, I can serve others," or "I must work because we need two incomes to survive." It means prayerfully discerning what fits for the family in any given season. It means listening to the truth about the current circumstances.

For example, a mother who is home all day, every day, with no outside interaction season after season could eventually find herself becoming less herself and less able to give to her family. Part of the way God designed us is for communion or community. Whether that is through earning an income at a job or volunteering outside of the home, connecting with others is part of our design.

Career and volunteer work both have the potential to increase our capacities in our primary vocation. A job outside the home helps support the family and, at the same time, allows a mother to use her God-given talents. Volunteer work to help others in need can do the same and even include members of the family. Finding the balance is the key.

Chancey M.

It's unfortunate when we let ourselves get dragged down into thinking that work is an obligation and service is slavery. The best and life-giving way to work and serve is out of love. When we can't find our love, we can work for the objective good that we are doing. If we still have our arms crossed, then we might get by with reminding ourselves, "I said I would."

In all these cases, I have discovered the power of the pale princess's motto: Whistle while you work! It's amazing how singing or whistling (even when forced—voice trembling—to start) automatically cheers us up and clears away the clouds just enough for us to remember our goal.

A quick, intimate visit to the Blessed Sacrament is even more effective. If you don't have the grace of living in the house of the King, a spiritual communion is accessible to all at every moment.

My good friend St. Therese and her disciple Mother Teresa help us to see that nothing is too small to contribute to the glory of God and the building up of his Kingdom.

Saint John Paul II reminds us, "Through work, man not only transforms nature, adapting it to his own needs, but he also achieves fulfilment as a human being and indeed, in a sense, becomes 'more a human being.'"

Sr. Holy Family

I think I mentioned that even into my twenties, my hero list did not include stay-at-home moms, and I had goals of accomplishing something "meaningful" with my life. Looking at my goals now, they are pretty simple; providing a happy and healthy home for my kids and hearing "well done" when my Savior calls me home into his embrace.

I hope for a hidden, simple life, and every day is like a challenge to grow in love and simplicity. Some moms are called by Our Lord to do more outside of their hidden sanctuary, but that is not a hope I have. Quite the contrary, actually. I'm so grateful for this simple calling to do little things with great love - no more for now, and no less.

The sacrament of confession is a literal lifesaver for keeping my selfish and self-centered tendencies in line, and I know that Holy Mass and the Eucharist are full of grace . . . otherwise how to explain the miracles of grace in these years of family life? God knows that our deepest happiness is found in him, not in achievements . . . and the absolute innocence, dependence, and cuteness of little ones can melt the hardest of hearts.

Katherine W.

CHAPTER SEVEN

Friendships and Community

She enjoys the profit from her dealings;
her lamp is never extinguished at night.

PROVERBS 31:18

Faithful friends are a sturdy shelter;
whoever finds one finds a treasure.

Faithful friends are beyond price,
no amount can balance their worth.

Faithful friends are life-saving medicine;
those who fear God will find them.

Those who fear the Lord enjoy stable friendship,
for as they are, so will their neighbors be.

SIRACH 6:14–17

MARNEE

*T*his theme has played such an immense role in my life. When I think of all the ways friendship and community have impacted me, my mind thinks: Thousands? Millions? I have had some valuable male friendships, but the vast majority have been female. To narrow this down to a chapter, I will focus on my friendships with women.

The mental image I get when I think about friendships and community is an image of being carried—lifted up, supported, helped to become who I am and get where I am today. It's not that I always recognized that or had a conscious concept of why I always sought to find, create, and foster community wherever I was. It was simply enough that I knew deeply that wholesome, authentic community is *good*.

One of God's attributes is *good*. So, you know when you encounter something that is true, beautiful, or good, it comes from God, and you will always benefit from it. And I think culturally, being raised in a family of nine children (and all the friends that come along with it), I was used to being in community and knew that I liked it.

I also learned from a young age that I needed close female friendships. Perhaps because I had not yet learned how to create close relationships with my own sisters or perhaps because I didn't have an older sister . . . who knows exactly. But I always wanted and needed my female friends.

Female friendships can be fraught with drama and hurt, perhaps more so than male friendships, since women know instinctively how to hurt each other. They can also be very cliquish, so there was some of that mixed in at times, too. Why young kids are often so mean to each other, I will never quite understand. My experiences in my early years made me afraid of most of my peers for a long time. Afraid of the judgmental or condescending looks, the once over of my thrift-store outfits, the whispering to a friend after seeing me, the fake friendliness, the laughing, or the questions like "Why are you so [something about my personality or presentation]?"

But there were always at least a few friends that I trusted completely, and as I got older and healed more, that number grew and grew. There are so many wonderful women I can call friends now. In fact, some of them are contributing to this book. My friends over the years have inspired me, taught me *so* much, encouraged me, kept me on the right path through tough times with their prayers, and poured so much time, energy and love into me. When I got married, I had ten bridesmaids and a handful of honorary bridesmaids. They represented what I considered the many women who got me to the altar and who are responsible for me marrying a man beyond my dreams.

It's not always easy to find community and good friendships, but when I have taken initiative to seek it out and appreciate those God puts in my life for that season, I have always felt there was success. And I honestly feel the community experience is much more enriched when there are a variety of vocational states and men and women involved - such a richer dynamic!

It saddens me considerably to see how female friendships have gotten confused in our culture today so that many do not experience this treasure that is so needed. It's not surprising this dynamic has been targeted, though—look at how much good it can do in the world!

As Brené Brown talks about in her book, *I Thought It Was Just Me But It Isn't*, we females can also carry a lot of shame around each other through judgment and comparison. Out of insecurity and weakness, we turn to tearing each other down to pull ourselves up in our own or others' estimation. This is toxic and detrimental and not really who we are made to be. Counteract the shame we all carry by speaking well of your fellow ladies. Admire them, respect them, hear their stories, be vulnerable with them. Don't assume you know someone until you've sat down and had the conversation with them.

We all wear facades; we all have things we want hidden. Though when they are brought to the light, not only do we find "it's not just me," we also find that typically, it was not worth hiding. Bring on the light! If God can search us and know us and still love us, let's not be afraid of our fellow women.

Different seasons of life may bring different kinds of friends. But hold on to the good ones if you can, no matter how divergent your situations may be. In this stage of life, most of my closest friends live in completely different states. Some of us met during a sweet time of community in a small neighborhood in the Bronx, NY, and over ten years later, we are still connected via the many wonderful virtual avenues we have at our disposal today.

When recently going through my miscarriages, I got loving notes, voice memos, phone calls, flowers, and meals from friends as close as a couple miles and as far as The Netherlands (my sister :). I certainly do wish we could all be in the same geographical area, but time and maturity show that true friendships stand the test of time and space, and your hearts are still close, even if you rarely get to see each other.

As one crazy twist of God's plan, one of my closest friends—a former classmate, who I have known for six years—met her future husband online from her home in Texas, and he lives in the same town in Michigan that I do! Another crazy part: This happened right after starting to write this book together . . . this friend is Jody! Now, that is cause for super friend celebration!!! You just never do know, do you?

JODY

Oh boy!! Where do I start? Catholic femininity, deeply rooted in the teachings of the Church, emphasizes the unique and complementary roles of women in fostering friendship and community. Women are often seen as the heart of the family and community, bringing warmth, compassion, and nurturing qualities that are essential for building strong, supportive relationships. Our femininity encourages us to form bonds based on mutual respect, love, and a shared commitment to faith. These friendships are not just social connections but spiritual partnerships that help individuals grow closer to God and live out their faith more fully. We play a vital role in creating a sense of belonging and unity.

Belonging and unity are what I've desired since my childhood because I didn't get that. I've had to start over completely several times in my life. I wasn't a military baby, but I've had my fair share of moving. It is important to understand that when our needs are not met, we will seek others to fill that hole. I have developed friendships from both places, first woundedness and later wholeness. Depending on which of these states we find ourselves in, the friends and community we surround ourselves with will either be life-giving or life-draining.

St. Augustine was a young boy stealing pears with his friends for the sake of sinning. I wonder if it was to avoid feeling alone. How many of us have found ourselves in unhealthy relationships for the sake of not feeling loneliness or isolation? I have, and it was a place of suffering until I realized that I needed to surround myself with those who are striving to be virtuous. Of course, we can be friends with those who don't share our values or faith. However, be prudent in this area to protect yourself from the worldly influences they bring.

If you have a strong friend group and faithful community, going out into the world to be the light to others is encouraged. It's when you're in a season of loneliness and isolation without a faith community that worldly influences will start to take root. This is a slow progression if you're not on guard. Remember, the enemy watches for opportunities to draw you away from God.

So, what's the answer? Lean into the loneliness and isolation. If you don't try to avoid the feelings but instead ask for God to enter that space and comfort you, then your emotional needs are met until God brings you the friendships and community you desire. It's not easy, and I encourage you to consult a spiritual director and therapist to help you during this time. Again, what is God inviting you into if he hasn't yet provided the friends and community you desire?

Marnee mentioned how she had mostly female friends, whereas I have had mostly male friends. It has been hard for me to relate to women and find the "right" women to be friends with. They had to be deep thinkers but not emotionally needy, tomboyish and straight to the point. I rejected my emotions because I viewed them as weak; they made me too vulnerable. It was emotionally safer if I denied my need to express my emotions.

We, as women, are created to be emotional because we facilitate intimacy. Over the past ten years, God has placed strong women who emulate Our Lady in my life. I have found great healing in getting close to the Blessed Mother since 2013. She has led me to the understanding of what it means to be feminine and how to seek those who embrace it as well.

Catholic femininity has taught me that friendship and community are about embodying the virtues of Mary, who is seen as the ultimate model of womanhood. Mary's humility, obedience, and unwavering faith serve as an inspiration for women to live out their roles with grace and dedication. In friendships, this means being a source of encouragement and support, always guiding others towards Christ. In the community, it means being a beacon of hope and love, working tirelessly to uplift those in need and create a more just and compassionate world. Through these actions, we as women live out our faith in tangible ways, making a profound impact on the lives of those around us.

My sisters in Christ, may you always feel seen and valued for your femininity. Seek those who can teach you how to embrace your femininity, grow in virtue, and enjoy the ride while discovering your true self. This is an adventure of femininity. Go big!!!

THE CONVERSATION CONTINUES

By my senior year of college, I had found myself in a close-knit group of like-minded Catholic friends. We supported one another authentically and ran with each other towards virtue and sainthood. I found my relationship with the Lord one of the strongest I had experienced. I felt so free with these friends because I had no reservations about being "that Catholic friend." I could just be me.

Towards the end of my senior year, I was terrified. We all had different plans for after graduation, and I started to grow anxious. If I didn't have anyone to ask to pray the Rosary with me, would I pray at all? How could I go back to going to Mass alone when I had experienced the beauty of going to Mass with people I loved?

I expressed all of these concerns to my spiritual advisor, Father Gino. After listening intently and a very long thoughtful silence, Father Gino simply told me, "Sometimes, Angie, Jesus gives you a lollipop. It's your favorite color and your favorite flavor. But then something happens, and Jesus has to take the lollipop away. You start to frown, and Jesus asks you, 'What do you love, me or the lollipop?'"

Initially, I was offended by this story—could I not love both? In our conversation, Father reminded me that, at its root, my relationship with my friends was rooted in Christ and that he was not going anywhere.

Friendships and community are such beautiful gifts from the Lord. I have had so many experiences where God used my friends to continue to remind me of his goodness and love for me. However, like all gifts from the Lord, they can be given and taken away. I will always cherish the friendships I made in college. Some of these friends I still talk to quite often, and some I have not spoken to since graduating. Though a little bittersweet, nothing truly good that comes from the Lord ever fully disappears. Through each of these friendships, the Lord has introduced me to a little more of his heart and continues to remind me to root everything in him.

Angie E.

Ecce quam bonum et quam jucundum habitare fratres in unum (Psalm 133) is the text of my favorite song by Palestrina. "See, how good and how pleasing it is for brothers to live together as one!" The value of friendship is incalculable, though it is not always easy and pleasant.

In the constitutions that I live by as a religious sister, it says (quoting Saint Benedict), "We must live fraternal charity: that is, outdo one another in showing honor (Romans 12:10); bear their weaknesses, both physical and spiritual, with unlimited patience; be eager to obey one another; seek not one's own good as much as one's neighbor's; practice true fraternal love; live always in the fear and love of God. Love your (superior) with true and humble charity; do not let anything come before Christ who will take all of us together to eternal life." Yes, good relationships built on Christ require cultivation and sacrifice. But the fruits we reap are great.

I love C.S. Lewis' quote about *philia*: "Friendship is unnecessary, like philosophy, like art. . . . It has no survival value; rather it is one of those things that give value to survival." What a blessing friendship and community life are.

Sr. Holy Family

Community should be a balance of intentionality and spontaneity. I've moved to new cities by myself several times, and it can take a while to find those solid, mutually enriching friendships we all desire. I've learned that it's important to actively seek out new friends in the pre-existing circles of a new community you join. Make yourself go to the young adult group at least once or twice, even if the activity they've chosen isn't your favorite. Introduce yourself to someone after church. Find a volunteer commitment you feel drawn to and engage with other volunteers.

It can feel like a huge effort at first, and it can be exhausting to meet so many new people. But widening your circle of acquaintances increases the chances of encountering those with whom you can cultivate deeper, intentional friendships later. If you just wait around for good friends to appear, they usually don't.

That said, the Holy Spirit works in marvelous and often unexpected ways to create community for you and through you. You'll meet people you're immediately drawn to and people you're immediately annoyed by. I've learned that God gives us acquaintance with all kinds of people, not just for our sake but for the sake of the Body of Christ. You deserve a loving and supportive community—and you are also called to help build that for others.

I've spent too many conversations at events looking around and wishing I could talk to someone else, when the person that most needs my attention is the one God has put in front of me at that moment. Even people you don't like at first can become dear to you in their own way. Learning this over and over through experience has helped me stop judging people by first impressions.

Honor others with your attention, reverence the unique human beings they are, and be open to the amazing places God can take your community through kindness and simple invitation.

Sarah D.

I have tried so often to solve my problems alone, in my own corner, in the rumination of my mind. And so often, I have experienced that most problems are quickly solved by just talking to a friend about them. Dear women, we are made for community! We do not need to—and we cannot—do it alone!

I have often had friends with whom I would be accountability partners, and we would both have some resolution, for example, spending less time on the phone; praying for twenty minutes every day, etc. A few times per week, we would check in with each other on how the resolutions were going and how we could pray for each other. Doing this together is so much easier than trying to do it on my own. It's as easy as that.

Let us not be afraid to reach out to one another and to be vulnerable. In the end, we are all struggling and often with the same things: how we look, our thoughts, emotions, longings, and comparison. What if we show to one another that we are struggling with these things and, through that, we can help and encourage one another?

Chiara D.

CHAPTER EIGHT

Fashion and Self-Expression

She makes her own coverlets;
fine linen and purple are her clothing.

Her husband is prominent at the city gates
as he sits with the elders of the land. . . .

Charm is deceptive and beauty fleeting;
the woman who fears the Lord is to be praised.

PROVERBS 31:22–23, 30

MARNEE

This topic seems to come up regularly in female discussions. Actually, the more we talk about it and how it impacts women, the more we discover how it impacts men as well.

I opened this book with the topic of femininity and beauty to set the stage for our conversations about life as a woman. I didn't open with fashion and self-expression, because these are not foundational; they are just one more aspect of feminine presentation and life experience.

This chapter has some overlap with the health chapter, maybe the chapter on romantic relationships, and the chapter on mental health. But I have it here standing alone, because I personally have found great significance in how the unique external beauty of women can be a force in the world when coupled with awareness, respect, and authenticity. Women, not men, were gifted with this beauty as a part of their person. Their beauty has such power that it has started and ended wars—if the ancient writings are believed— can cause men to overcome the greatest obstacles to obtain or even glimpse it, and on and on.

We have a wonderful power and gift. Yet, as they say, with great power comes great responsibility. Fashion and self-expression can be tools for sharing your God-given beauty with others! It took me a long time to undo the perspective that fashion is superficial, purely oversexualized, or at the very least not attainable for the average midwestern country girl (aka me). Also, that it would be forever out of my price range.

Fashion can have all those aspects, but at its foundation, I see it as an art form that is especially crafted for highlighting every type of human beauty. And it can be done on a budget with creativity and patience.

I have my time living in New York City to thank for learning to understand fashion more authentically. If legions of women are giving their time and paychecks for it, what underlying good so draws them? My wardrobe growing up was baggy Walmart and mismatched Goodwill. Partly because it was cheap (well, that was honestly the main reason), partly because it was low maintenance, and partly because I was shamed into being afraid or embarrassed of my own body.

I had absorbed the messages "Hide it!" "Don't attract attention!" Especially from those dangerous men who all "only want one thing." Those poor, good men who are trying to figure out how to tell a woman she is attractive are terrified to say the wrong thing lest they get accused of sexual harassment. The fewer dirty-minded blokes out there who actually sexually harass women on a regular basis should be locked up. They are ruining it for the good ones.

Being in New York brought on a slow liberation of seeing fashion and dressing well as an important part of being fully yourself. It takes a while to identify your color palette, body type, preferred materials and cuts, and the sources of inexpensive fashion, but I find it worth it. And it doesn't rule out Walmart and Goodwill! Each of us will have a different way of expressing ourselves through our appearance, plus practical limitations. So, you do you.

The journey of being able to express your own femininity in an authentic and complimentary way may take years. It may also require healing of wounds and negative perceptions about being a woman, being beautiful, being desirable, and being able to believe your intrinsic value is not altered by anything you do, say, or wear. Let's face it—even the most celebrated model or actress has days when she does not feel beautiful. I've heard she has even more of those days than most women.

As tricky a subject as it is, a book for Catholic women dealing with fashion and appearance probably needs a note on modesty. Yikes! This is a trigger word for so many of us. Why is it that so few of us were raised with a healthy understanding in the area of "modesty" and another phrase generally said with a negative connotation, "purity culture?" For most, these terms carry a sense of shame and judgment around our bodies as women and the understanding of our sexuality.

In case your parents or church community didn't communicate this to you, your body is so good! Your sexuality is so good! The shame, confusion, and rebellion around our bodies and sexual identity we see pervasive today likely have grown from destructive seeds related to modesty and purity culture planted in the name of God and in the language of fear.

I have thought (and continue thinking) about how I will speak to my own daughter (currently two years old) about her body, dress, and sexuality. The script is still in process, but the current version reads something like: "It's wonderful to be a woman! Every part of you is so beautiful. Some parts God made especially beautiful for bringing you and your husband close in marriage. Those parts we save in joyful anticipation for what is to come! It may be hard to fully understand before marriage, but it will make sense then, and you'll be glad you did."

Also, "Let's try our best to find clothes you like and that add to your natural beauty! I know these are some colors that look great on you—which ones do you like? I'm not a big fan of leggings out in public (unless they are under a dress), but let's find pants that are comfortable for playing in. We'll try out some hairstyles over time to see what complements your beautiful face, and you can let me know what you think of them."

I can tell when a woman has some sense of what compliments her and adds beauty to her presentation and the artist in me rejoices. We can never have too much beauty in the world! My heart goes out to the woman who was never taught or who unconsciously hides her beauty out of a protective fear. She is likely not presenting her truest self, and she likely does not recognize the full extent of her God-given beauty.

If we ever look at ourselves and don't feel beautiful, it can bring our whole day down. And the crazy thing is, we can feel this way even when we do the same things as yesterday, and yesterday we felt good about it! We women certainly know how sensitive this topic is, so immaturity, insecurity, or jealousy can have girls making pointed jabs at others that highlight and criticize certain aspects of their appearance.

This does not have to be a competition, ladies. We are not peacocks vying for attention. How true it seems to be that when a woman carries a heavy anxiety about appearance in her daily life, it often has more to do with how she thinks she will be perceived by other women than by men. We love our friends, but low self-esteem tells us they are all super beautiful and we are ugly. And everyone else is noticing it, too. Right?

My husband knows my insecurities and has been highlighting the beauty he sees in me regularly for about four years now. I still have a hard time taking it in sometimes. So much internal woundedness to work through. But I am much closer to a place of recognizing that while every woman has beauty to share (and that includes me!) there is no need for ranking. Comparison is so subjective as to be entirely useless. Plus, I have learned for a long time now through the eyes of men who love their women, that each of us in our womanhood has a captivating quality, no matter what our external presentation is or how we feel about it.

JODY

*F*ashion has never been my strong suit (pardon the pun). I don't care about the latest fashions or anything related to them. I wear what I classify as elegant-edgy. What I am concerned about is how I am presenting myself. I try to express my personality through my wardrobe while practicing modesty. Sweatsuit outfits or activewear are my go-to. You never know when you're going for a hike or off-roading.

What the Catholic Church has taught me about fashion and self-expression is that it is deeply intertwined with the belief that the body is a temple of the Holy Spirit and a reflection of God's image. This perspective encourages women to dress in a way that honors their dignity and the sacredness of their bodies. Fashion emphasizes that clothing should enhance, rather than detract from, a woman's inherent worth and the virtues she embodies. It can reveal the unique and unrepeatable nature of each individual. Inspired by St. John Paul II's Theology of the Body, this approach to fashion acknowledges that the body and soul are inseparable, and what we wear can manifest our inner selves. By choosing clothing that reflects their personality and faith, women can communicate their identity and values to the world. This form of self-expression is seen as a way to glorify God and inspire others through the beauty and creativity inherent in each person.

Our femininity places a significant emphasis on the virtue of modesty, viewing it as essential for maintaining purity. Modesty in dress and behavior is seen as a way to protect the intimate center of the person, ensuring that one's appearance and actions reflect inner purity and honor the sacredness of the body. The responsibility to be modest is also linked to the call to live a chaste life.

Modesty helps to guard against lust and objectification, fostering an environment where individuals are valued for their whole person rather than just their physical appearance.

My mother taught me modesty indirectly. She struggled with her weight and found clothes that looked nice and covered problem areas. This gave me a sense of finding what I was comfortable with while making a statement of who I was. Remember, I am more of a tomboy, so I rejected "girly girl" clothes when I was younger, and having elegant-edgy clothes was not on my radar until recently. Only in the past ten years have I found what works for me (and it's ever- changing).

I'm sure when you are doing your yearly purging of the closest, you think, "What in the world was I thinking when I bought that?" or "Wow, this doesn't fit like it used to," or even better, "When and where did I get this?" It has been my experience that fashion and self-expression go hand in hand. Be curious about new patterns, designs, and styles. You are evolving daily into the woman God created you to be. Allow that expression to be seen and embraced. Have fun while doing it, and bring a good friend who will say, "Mmmm, no. That's not for you," with all the love in her heart.

Shop, discover, and embrace who you are in God's eyes!!!

THE CONVERSATION CONTINUES

One of my favorite play activities when I was younger was flipping through a coloring book my mom had made for me. On each page, my mom drew pictures of dolls by hand in different outfits. I loved seeing my mom's creations so much that I didn't even color in the book; I wanted so badly to preserve the art my mom had made.

A few years later, my parents bought me a Barbie Flip and Fold fashion toy. In this toy, a Barbie mold lay in the bottom of a folder. On the top part, there was a cut-out that fit the silhouette of Barbie's body. Based on how you folded the different fabrics that came with the set, you could make hundreds of different combinations for Barbie to wear. I absolutely adored playing fashion designer, even finding different objects around the house I could use. I felt so creative and accomplished when I made Barbie a wedding dress from a few table napkins!

I have always loved to play with fashion. The mixing and matching of fabrics, color blocking, playing with shapes and accessories—all of it makes a part of my brain very happy. When I was fifteen, I became enthralled by the most beautiful piece of self-expression I had ever seen—the mantilla, or the chapel veil. After a year of praying and researching, I resolved that on my sixteenth birthday, which happened to fall on a Sunday that year, I, too, would start the practice of veiling.

It has been fourteen years since I started veiling, and I still see the practice as part of my self-expression. Often, the way that we present ourselves reveals the movements of our hearts. Somewhere in my research, I read that the Bible mentions that the beauty of a woman lies in her hair. When a woman veils during the Mass or Eucharistic Adoration, she claims her beauty but is saying, "I am beautiful, but look at what is most beautiful—the Eucharist!" I still love fashion, but something I have learned since starting veiling is that, as the Psalms express, whatever I wear on my body is most comfortable when it matches that dignity and strength that God clothes me with.

Angie E.

I remember writing to the sisters I lived with for five months during my vocational discernment. I had just received the habit of our institute a few days before. It was one of those spontaneous emails in which you yourself don't even know what you're about to say. I typed: "Finally my reflection shows who I am inside!" Never thought I'd quote *Mulan* as a nun, but she really hit my exact feelings.

Many people who knew me before entering the convent might have been surprised (and indeed some of them expressed their shock) at the idea of me wearing the same thing every day. My Aunt Deb used to call me the "fashion diva." And yet, it was amazing the relief I felt at truly being able to express myself: I am his. Nothing else is more important.

Sr. Holy Family

Modesty is beautiful. And I don't just mean that in some spiritual or abstract way. It should actually look beautiful. If modesty isn't beautiful, then you are doing it wrong.

Both men and women crave beauty. Instead, we are surrounded by either ugliness or sexiness, neither of which is fulfilling or attractive. Women used to wear hats and gloves just to go out. Now, the standard, such as some leggings outfits, seems deficient of true feminine presentation.

With whatever budget you have, buy the nicest, classiest things you can afford. Better to have fewer quality pieces that will last than a lot of cheaply made "fast fashion." Don't be afraid to wear a skirt or a dress, even to the grocery store. I often joke with my kids when they compliment my outfit, "Well, *somebody* has to make this housewife thing look good."

Dignified beauty draws the best out of others. I can't tell you how many compliments and thanks I have received when wearing something as simple as a skirt and a sweater. I've had men go out of their way to open doors or reach for an item on the top shelf for me. I had one guy at the meat counter thank me for looking nice, then tell me that he and his buddy were just complaining that morning about people not caring anymore and looking like slobs. When he handed me my package, he said, "Give 'em hell." As he was a young man and richly tattooed, I figured that was high praise.

But beauty is a taste of heaven—it was created by God. And every time Mother Mary appears, she is beautiful. So, no matter what season of life you are in, resist the urge to be frumpy or sloppy. Dress in accord with your dignity—it will help both you and others.

Jenny B.

It can be hard to practice or teach modesty in a culture that loves the sensual and the erotic. One of my spiritual directors gave me the best advice on modesty in dress that I have ever received. She simply said, "Tight enough to know you are a woman but loose enough to know you are a lady."

Vicky T.

CHAPTER NINE

Healing Traumas and Mental Health

She is not concerned for her household when it snows—all her charges are doubly clothed.

PROVERBS 31:21

For I know well the plans I have in mind for you . . . plans for your welfare and not for woe, so as to give you a future of hope. When you call me, and come and pray to me, I will listen to you. When you look for me, you will find me. Yes, when you seek me with all your heart, I will let you find me . . . and I will change your lot.

JEREMIAH 29:11–14

All the absurdity of which mankind's foolishness and blindness are capable is caught up in God's loving omnipotence. He is able to fit even the absurd into his plan of salvation and thereby give it meaning.

WILFRID STINISSEN

MARNEE

There is a saying going around, "You're not responsible for what was done to you, but you are responsible for your own healing." That can be a tough realization. It's not fair. But it's true. Part of coming into adulthood involves shifting responsibility for why we do what we do from our parents (or others) to ourselves.

Healing from a traumatic childhood takes time and has many facets. For instance, we first need to acknowledge what was done, through a long period of reflecting, grieving, letting go, and accepting. Then, we take on the long-term work of healing ourselves—from experiences that were not our fault and maybe some that were.

Our relationship with God may be one that helps us tremendously here, or it may be another area in need of exploration and healing. Of course, wherever we are at with God, he is always good with us. He's always helping and involved, even if we are not sure what to do with him right now.

I believe we are all touched by mental illness today, whether in ourselves or someone else. If we have it ourselves, it's likely because someone in our childhood had it first. Some grew up with it, and it is recognizably a part of their story from the beginning. Others may be severely shaken by its unexpected presence later on. I have sometimes wondered which is ultimately harder to deal with: always living with it and by adulthood wrestling through the effects with deep familiarity or living the first part of your life barely being aware of its existence in the world only to be rocked by it appearing (or being recognized) later in your life when you're feeling safe and established.

If mental illness has long been a part of your life story, whether in your family or yourself, you may be more comfortable talking about it. This is a significant factor. It means that you probably have some sort of community who knows about it, you've likely sought help for it, and you are educated about it to some extent. In these ways, the stigma is lessened, and you are not alone.

If, however, you encounter it for the first time later in life, it can be deeply jarring. It can take the foundation right out from under you. You have to make a choice. Either you are going to enter into understanding the reality of mental illness—that it can't be willed or prayed away and it makes deep, complex impacts on everyone around it—or you will try to hold onto the idea that it is just a person being weak or sinful, and if they would just get it together, we could all go on as before. If you choose to face it as reality, you likely have to rethink many things about your life and humanity that shake your view of the world. Ultimately, you will find humility, empathy, and a much deeper connection with the struggle of your fellow man.

I never thought I would end up working in the field of mental health. Psychology was an area of lowest interest when deciding what to study post–high school. Perhaps because it was so profoundly embedded in every aspect of my growing up, or maybe it just felt too heady and passive while I wanted to do something more interactive and adventurous.

But, after a handful of academic milestones, at thirty, just as I was moving from New York back to my home state of Michigan, God lined everything up in an irresistible way, and I was on my way to getting a master's in clinical mental health counseling. There were three powerful fruits of getting that degree: three years of intensive self-work, a powerhouse group of life-long friends, and a very solid, integrated education in how to be a good counselor.

Has everyone seen *Good Will Hunting*? The scene with Robin

Williams and Matt Damon at the climactic moment of healing inspires all aspiring counselors. How powerful it is to help another person really hit the nail on the head and launch into a freedom of healing and authentic identity.

When I see clients who are practicing Catholics with a strong (and mostly positive) connection to their faith, I notice that their healing process is exponentially faster. When they come in with overwhelming problems, in an astonishingly short time, they find they are able to manage things with resources on their own (with God), no longer needing regular therapy.

There is a lot of debate about what is causing a growing epidemic of mental health issues. I don't give too much attention to statistics or trending articles, as too many numbers and detached reports tend to very easily lose sight of the individual person and their specific situation. Whether we look at anxiety in young people, the rise in ADHD diagnoses in recent years, divorce rates, sexual abuse frequency, the increase in suicides—all very heavy realities—each one represents not only a person but a family, a friend group, and a community impacted.

So, what do you do if trauma, mental health issues, or experiences with others who suffer from mental health are a part of your story? That's okay. There are so many good resources these days and so much hope. It doesn't define you, but it sure does have a part in making you who you are today, which can become something positive and powerful.

God never wants trauma to happen. He didn't design us to suffer from anxiety, depression, or OCD. It takes a lot of work to manage these symptoms over time. Perhaps it's the hand we have been dealt, and so, just as we care about the health of our bodies, keep our teeth brushed every day, and work on that prayer life, we also put effort into our mental and emotional health.

Try it on your own first. Pray, reflect, journal, walk and talk to trusted, self-aware individuals. Read, watch content, feel the emotions, and ask the big questions. If you find yourself coming up against blocks or others give you the feedback that more work is needed, take it to the next level. Find a professional to talk with, likely a therapist/counselor (master's level) or psychologist (doctorate level). There are ways to look for Catholic ones (see resources), and it may take a while to find that right fit. It may take longer if you need to use insurance or have limited income. Keep trying.

If you need some basic meds to take the edge off of your anxiety or depression, your primary physician can usually prescribe those. If you need a higher level of medication care, find a psychiatrist with whom you feel comfortable. You'll probably still need a counselor as well.

You don't have to share your mental health journey with everyone. I hope you have some trusted individuals who can help air out your thought processes. Sharing can be very helpful, but too much vulnerability or overexposure can increase symptoms if underlying traumas are not well-processed and resolved. And even though you are going on this journey, don't assume others on the journey will have the same experiences or outcomes as you.

We are each so different. As a counselor, I see that continually. A host of people may come in with anxiety, but each one has a very different story behind it and needs their own particular approach to healing.

It is an honor to be invited into each client's life, and I enjoy getting to know them, especially identifying their particular strengths that contribute to their healing. It's a wonderful thing to see someone grow in freedom through their hard work and perseverance, along with the ever-present grace of God. I can tell someone has found solid footing when they recognize God is a good God who only gives good things, when they can see themselves in the greater context of the world around them, and when they no longer carry their wounds as a burden on their back but simply as a challenging part of their life that they work at with consistency and humility.

JODY

I want to say to everyone reading this book, I am so *sorry* you were mistreated, abused, and hurt by someone. That mark on your heart is real, and it matters!!!! You matter, and you are worth the time it will take to heal from your wounds.

There is so much to say on this topic that I'm having trouble knowing what to focus on. So here goes . . .

I was a cardiovascular intensive care nurse in the first nine years of my nursing career. During this time, I took care of the sickest patients. There were moments I got to witness miracles where you could feel the Holy Spirit working. I also felt the Spirit working at the pregnancy care center while working with women contemplating abortion.

Let me paint the picture of the deep effects of trauma on mental health: you get a phone call that your loved one was hit by a semi-truck driving sixty miles per hour. You rush to the hospital to find out they are in surgery and won't be out for another seven hours. You wait.

Then you are told you can visit them for a short period of time but that they will be under controlled sedation until they are stable. You turn the corner, and you see your loved one in a full body cast, a breathing tube and other tubes connected to every body part, multiple IV pumps, alarms going off constantly, and medical staff working hard to keep them alive with potentially lethal medications.

Would you tell your loved one after two days, "Hey, why are you still lying there? Get over it and stop feeling sorry for yourself. You can't take too much time off work. I can't believe you are like this." This list goes on.

I don't think most people would. Why? Because we hold more empathy, understanding, and reasonable expectations when we visually see someone suffering.

Now change the picture to a person who appears to be physically healthy but is experiencing what I just described on the inside. You can't see it, so there are often no graces or understanding when it comes to someone dealing with chronic or acute trauma. But for the person suffering, until the trauma is fully processed, their bodies will remember it and respond in a negative way, keeping them from flourishing or having healthy relationships. It is the undercurrent for most impulsive behaviors, anxieties, depression, and anger. Listen to what your body is telling you, and you will find the wound.

I tell my couples all the time that it's not about the garbage or shoes under the table or toothpaste in the bathroom sink. If we dig, there is meaning behind why little things irritate you or why you have a short fuse. I encourage you to take time to notice what your body is telling you by taking a deep breath, locating the sensation (by doing a head-to-toe body scan), and then asking yourself, "What is the emotion I am feeling? When did I feel something similar or the same in the past?" Wait for the answer. It might take a few minutes. The Holy Spirit will respond. Just go with it and see where he leads you. You might be surprised at the answer. Breathe and lean into it.

In my profession, I focus on helping people process their trauma. We all have experienced it in some way. Big "T" traumas could be life- threatening: natural disasters, war/combat, mental, physical, verbal, or sexual abuse, attachments to caretakers/parents, violence, or terrorism. Little "t" traumas are non-life-threatening but could still cause emotional or psychological stress—for instance, bullying, harassment, chronic stress, emotional neglect, minor accidents or injuries, etc.

The fact of the matter is, whatever kind of trauma you have experienced and haven't processed, it acts like a slow-growing infection. From the time you were conceived, your body has collected information to keep it safe. The body will signal danger but doesn't know if it's perceived or real. For instance, it cannot differentiate between a bear chasing you or someone posing an emotional threat. Your body will have the same response. Therefore, the goal would be for our intellect and reason to communicate with our bodies/emotions. Emotions/feelings give us information for our survival but ought not take control.

Most people will shut off the emotional side to not feel negative feelings. Because trauma lives in our emotions, we want to avoid them. God created all emotions for a reason. In order for you to flourish, learning how to honor and balance your emotions with your intellect gives glory to God's creation that lives within you.

Let me spend a moment on self-regulation, since it is key to having healthy relationships, especially with God. Emotional self-regulation is the ability to manage and respond to your emotions in a healthy and productive way. You can *be real* with yourself, God, and in all your relationships. Emotional regulation is first taught by your caretakers or parents through modeling, guidance, and practice. Here are some ways it is developed:

1. Modeling behavior: Parents and caregivers demonstrate self-regulation by managing their own emotions and reactions in front of children.
2. Setting clear expectations: Establish rules and routines so that children understand what is expected of them and develop a sense of security.
3. Teaching coping strategies: Help children manage their emotions with techniques like deep breathing, counting to ten, or using words to express feelings.
4. Providing positive reinforcement: Praise and reward children when they successfully regulate their emotions to encourage them to continue using these skills.
5. Providing a safe environment: Create a supportive and understanding environment where children feel safe to express their emotions and learn from their experiences.

The caretaker or parent should strive for consistency in responding to the child's needs. We are flawed and not perfect. However, you should seek to be available to your child's emotional safety and needs more often than not. However, most people are not taught this and can't tolerate their children's emotions because they can't tolerate their own. If any of these key components are missing, I suggest investing time with the Lord and a good therapist to show you where and why this might be. Generational trauma is passed down until someone in the family breaks the cycle.

In my own trauma, the Lord led me through breaking many generational trauma cycles. I was floored to realize how much and how deep abandonment from my father influenced my worldview, relationships, how I see myself, and how it contributed to my attachment style. Though this was reflected most in my romantic relationships, friendship can give us information about our trauma in a general way. Patterns are developed when we are children and will play out in all of our relationships.

Healing trauma is not easy. It takes time and requires patience. The process is not linear, and discovering how your defenses work and why it can be jolting at times. However, God wants you to flourish and brings you close. The process of redemption on the cross was brutal. Jesus's passion shows us his love and how to honor your emotions without losing control. Take some time to reflect on Scripture, where Jesus showed his emotions and the many references to human emotion in the Old Testament. Here are some examples:

1. At the wedding at Cana (John 2)
2. When he fed the 5,000 (Matthew 14)
3. When he cleansed the temple (Matthew 21; Mark 11; John 2)
4. At the death of Lazarus (John 11)
5. In the Garden of Gethsemane (Matthew 26; Mark 14)

Remember, it is normal to have emotions, both positive and negative. Most people find it difficult to experience the negative. These feelings are not fun, and the fear of getting stuck there or playing the victim causes one to dismiss their hurts and prevents a person from honoring themselves. Likewise, trauma could cause someone to develop extreme emotions that have no boundaries and are out of control. Again, there is a reason for this, and seeking help will provide answers. The more you are aware of yourself, the more you will flourish and become like the image of Christ.

You are created for more than how the world treats you. You decide how to handle your trauma and healing. Processing the wounds frees you to live a fuller life by making you whole again. Jesus created you whole and wants to give you an abundant life. He can't do that if we put up defenses and strive for self-reliance.

Protecting yourself as a child was needed. Now, you are an adult, and you have choices. How do you want to live your life from this day forward? When will you take the time to honor yourself so you can honor others? I hope you will start today!! You are worth it, and I pray for your healing and freedom to flourish. God is waiting.

THE CONVERSATION CONTINUES

I can remember the first time I heard someone suggest that I had "wounds." I was so offended, so confused. After all, I thought, "Do I have to blame my parents, who may have been the people to create some of those wounds, in order to be a whole person today?"

Little did I know that we are *all* wounded people travelling through this life, which includes all our baggage, good and bad. Examining our wounds may hurt temporarily. It's tough to revisit painful moments in our lives. But when we bring our wounds to the Lord and vulnerably show them to him, only then can he do his most miraculous work in us.

Now, a decade after those initial thoughts about woundedness, I recognize that one of the best decisions I have ever made was to commit to regular therapy. In this safe environment, I can vulnerably come face to face with my woundedness and the traumas in my life that caused it and encounter it with love and compassion, all in the arms of a loving Father. Whether you find the little girl who was sometimes neglected or the young woman who wanted to be noticed for her talents, acknowledging her, embracing her, and loving her is the only way to heal her.

Chancey M.

John Paul II had some great words for all of us, but the one phrase that has had *the most* impact on me personally was "There is so much wasted suffering in this world" (or words to that effect). This is so true! Physical suffering is very obvious, but emotional suffering is just as painful, if not more so.

How do most people react to physical suffering? Pain relievers seem to be everywhere! Let's explore how most people react to emotional suffering. First, there are as many kinds of emotional suffering as there are people in this world (past, present and future). One could be bullying from those considered friends or being slighted by one's closest family members. Another kind is experienced when seeing a beloved away from their loving God and living in a life of sin. For some, the deeper agony of an unexplainable sadness and depression can sometimes seem overwhelming.

There is a level of emotional suffering experienced by each person. Yet, how do we react? Some people react with equally hurtful anger and bitterness to the perpetrator (where innocent little ones nearby often can also receive great hurt). Some react with a deeper journey into the pitiful world of inner despair. Some have other reactions to an emotional suffering that are equally dark and bring them to the opposite of healing.

Some, however, learn how to follow Jesus in those most challenging moments through forgiveness. "Take up your cross and follow me." These are the moments where we take up the cross and follow him . . . the moments of suffering where we either have a physical ailment or an opportunity to practice forgiveness. This is suffering not wasted but used to console Jesus and save souls. By doing so, the innocent bystanders are also then blessed by our suffering and the willingness to offer it out of love. In this case, our suffering is not wasted or without purpose but takes on a deep meaning and beauty and brings such glory and consolation to God! He is so good . . . because if we even try to offer our suffering like this, he blesses us with the deep joy that he promised to his disciples.

The movie *Life Is Beautiful* with Roberto Benigni is probably one of the most touching movies that I've ever seen. I still think about it years after watching it . . . for the reason of joy that was brought in a situation of darkness, out of love for his son. Roberto

Benigni (director and actor) actually sat down with John Paul II and viewed it with him during the pre-screening stage. John Paul II himself spoke highly of this movie.

Roberto stars as a goofy, fun-loving man who eventually marries the love of his life. They have one son, who is the center of their love, which continues after marriage. Unfortunately, this poor man is a Jew and is sent to a concentration camp along with his uncle and his son. Though his wife is not a Jew, she voluntarily enters the concentration camp as another prisoner to be near her family.

Throughout the darkness, his humor remains. At the beginning of this movie, he was humorous by nature. As the movie progressed, however, he kept his sense of humor in order to protect his son from the evil surrounding them. Although this movie seems so small, in my eyes, this movie portrayed an example of huge sacrifice and love unlike any other I've ever seen.

In the end, his love prevails over the evil that was trying to destroy the people's hope and any love in their hearts. His son maintains innocence and joy even in the center of a concentration camp because of his dad's great love and perseverance, using the sense of humor that God had given him.

The father's humor was like a gift given by God, preparing him for this most difficult part of his life. And what a success, because, "No greater love has anyone than he who lays his life down for a friend!" In this case, his own son and wife. And, of course, she lays down her life for her husband and son as well by freely choosing to enter the pit of evil in that camp out of love for them. The movie isn't completely perfect . . . his goofy humor is at times a bit over the top, but not enough to make it any less than one of my favorite movies of all time.

One last wrap-up on what John Paul II said about suffering.

We can see Mary as the model of someone who definitely did not waste any suffering she endured. Probably the greatest suffering for her was to see Jesus suffer. Instead of growing in bitterness or anger or feelings of revenge that many people may feel when they see their loved ones hurt unjustly, she lived the example of forgiveness, acceptance, trust in God, and hope for Jesus's promises to be fulfilled soon. As a result, she only grew in her all-beautiful love for God and great holiness that must have radiated to everyone who saw her, especially those who knew her intimately.

I thought of so many ways one can suffer emotionally, because there's truly a zillion, just as the number of people God has made and the days that each one lives. How beautiful life would suddenly be if we could all learn to respond with forgiveness.

Katherine W.

Trauma and mental health are such sensitive topics. This is not only because we are still working through the taboos extant in our society around the topics but because, most often, our stories come from a murky place somewhere between the trauma itself and actual healing.

And what is healing? Is it forgetting the trauma enough to move forward? Is it being able to think about the trauma without repulsion? What does healing mean? I have to honestly say that I don't fully know yet.

In the past year, I (and my family) endured a trauma that rocked us to our core. It broke a piece of me that I never imagined could be broken. Being pregnant and then having a second child within this time made my heart even more vulnerable. I cannot describe the agony that this experience caused for all involved. Navigating boundaries, loss of trust, and a deep anger with a persistent voice convincing me that fear was the only thing left in my marriage.

I cannot give details of the specific trauma, but it broke me—it broke us. I remember driving one day and just thinking to myself how fickle human love truly is. How fickle I truly am. If I could have run away in those moments, maybe I would have. If it was plausible to start a new life over again on another planet, maybe I would have.

The darkest thoughts imaginable plagued me. I'm ashamed to say those things out loud—but they are the truth. What I found at every turn was that people are disturbed by saying these things out loud. I was shocked at how uncomfortable those I loved were with my and my spouse's pain. But we all do this don't we? With good intentions, we say, "Don't cry!" or "But it wasn't really them!" or we try to find the "silver lining." Hearing these phrases is exhausting. It is alienating. I don't believe it is God.

I found and am still working on seeing that God sits with us in the lion's den. He is quietly present as we sob brokenly, ugly, looking at the sky, wishing for time to stop. He wants us in our raw moments, in the moments where we have to admit that without his grace, we are ash.

The truth is, I am not fully healed, and I don't know that a hole like that can be filled. But I think something deeper and more real can be built around and grown over it. I used to think it was amazing to see a couple married for fifty-plus years dancing out on the floor at yet another small-town wedding. I smiled and prayed silently for it to be me someday.

Now I can see a little more clearly: you don't get to those places without scars, without burdens, and without stress or trauma. Perseverance, faithfulness, and a promise are sometimes all we have pulling us through. But those virtues are everything. They are proof that more exists within us than our biology and cells. God made us immortal. And he made us tenderly - he cannot abandon us and will not.

I am still putting this puzzle back together. But it looks different now—and I guess that is okay with me. With this realization, I have finally stepped forward into healing—even in just a small way. We absolutely must be present to people in their darkest moments. I want to urge all of us to hold others in their sorrow and allow the anger, fear, and hurt to rise and fall. We need to allow the poison to seep out so God can fill the spaces with something far greater and make beautiful pathways out of our scars.

Raechel W.

I have to admit, I was always very skeptical when people would talk about traumas. I thought "you with your traumas; don't blame everything on that" or "well, I don't have such big traumas, so that doesn't apply to me." Well, blessed are those who are being made humble enough by God to realize they also have traumas.

Yes, life has been teaching me that actually, we all have traumas or, as I like to call them, wounds. And it makes us so much more free to flourish when we discover them and go through them so that they can heal.

It doesn't necessarily mean that we have experienced abuse. But we all have places in our lives, in our hearts, where we have experienced a certain lack of love that has caused a wound. Through our wounds, we started to have mechanisms in us to "make up" for this love. Over recent years, I have been diving deep into my childhood, and thanks to great counselors and online courses, I have been able to discover unexpressed emotions and unresolved conflicts I am still carrying in me and how they hold me back from flourishing and from experiencing the love of others.

Women, it may take a bit of courage, but I would recommend to everyone: go deep in yourself, with the guidance of a trusted friend/counselor/spiritual director, and discover how much more free to love and to be loved you can become!

Chiara D.

CHAPTER TEN

Healthy Living and Self-Care

She girds herself with strength;
she exerts her arms with vigor.

PROVERBS 31:17

MARNEE

The good news is that there is *so* much content out there right now about how to be healthy and live well. The challenging part is . . . how do we sort through it and figure out what is right for me, the individual?

We know that giving attention to our health is important. We can look to the loving design of our bodies by our creator to see they merit great care and consideration. We also know we feel better—more confident, more happy, etc.—when we are healthy and our system is running smoothly. For those who have suffered chronic illnesses or had sudden health losses, "your health is everything" resonates loudly.

Health is also a tricky subject for women these days. Maybe it's the stress of feeling like we have to be on top of one more thing in life, and that thing (health) is just not always as easily controlled as we would hope, so we "fail" at it sometimes and feel weighed down by that. Maybe health in the female mind is also so closely linked to appearance. If someone is not deemed medically healthy, they may have trouble talking about health. If someone is deemed medically healthy, they may have trouble finding an interested ear if they still have physical concerns.

I tend to consider myself healthy, but when I list all the times I've been to the doctor, had to go to the ER, or had blood tests, I am usually quite surprised at the variety of uncomfortable medical encounters I've had in my young and "healthy" life. Boy, it's no fun being in a hospital. (Though I am starting to understand why seasoned moms consider hospital delivery time a vacation experience—someone else serving you good food, doing your laundry, taking care of the cleaning, while you are resting in bed. :-)) Anyway, it's so humbling, and sometimes humiliating, having all the examinations, pokes, questions, hospital gowns with the open back, assortment of clinicians, sleep deprivation, and on and on. Those who endure this on a regular basis have surely been put through the trial by fire.

Avoiding such situations is a great motivation to try our best to stay healthy, but there are others as well. There is also the strong and mysterious body-soul connection. Eating crummy food can bring on a crummy mood. Not getting physical movement can bring a lethargy of mind and heart too. Caring about your health is an investment that communicates you care about yourself, which reinforces your value to yourself and to others. Taking care of your appearance and health sends a strong message to your spouse, and he generally deeply appreciates it. Your decisions are not just for yourself but also for those deeply connected to you.

My husband tells me how much he values that I take care of myself, and I tell him the same. Don't get me wrong, when he first tried to delicately mention it in our dating period, my don't-reduce-me-to-my-appearance-or-tell-me-how-I-need-to-look alarms went off, and we had to have a number of conversations to sort through that culture-induced filter. I'm glad we did. That lens is really not mine, nor is it rooted in goodness. The fact is, I appreciate that my husband cares so much for his health and appearance too, but I shouldn't have the pass to say that while he gets silenced as an oppressive chauvinist when he says it to me. The dance of attraction and bonding within a marriage is vital and strong while also sensitive. To take care of yourself with the motivation of showing care for your spouse is a deeply beautiful thing.

I recently got a diagnosis of Hashimoto's and began embarking on that long-feared road of gluten and dairy-free eating. I salute those who have carried that burden their whole life long. Turns out, as others have discovered before me, that it actually becomes very motivating to just feel better on a regular basis (though that transition away from sugar was grueling for about a month).

As my husband and I age, health becomes more and more of a priority, and it gives us peace of mind knowing we are both doing what we can to stay around for each other and our children as long as possible. We know we don't have complete control, and suffering will always be a part of life, but I suppose we are just trying to be good stewards of the coins we've been given, to apply the parable in an interesting way.

As with all good things in life, we struggle for that delicate balance when it comes to taking care of ourselves. I'm a therapist, and I'm continually advocating for self-care with my clients, but that never includes causing hurt to another person, wielding your need for care as a weapon, or sliding down into self-centered mode, where your needs always trump anyone else's.

I'm guessing many who are reading this book deal more often with the other extreme, though, where thinking about "my needs" feels selfish and possibly prideful. We have definitely heard loud and clear that pride is our #1 enemy in the Catholic Christian life, and it sure gets brought up a lot. Whether it's our own mind, our confessor, or our overzealous friends and family, avoiding pride can turn into a chokehold that leaves little room for anything aside from sacrifice of our identity and humanity for the service of others. No good, ladies.

God made us equal, yes? Then your needs are just as important as those of the people in your life. It's simple math. If they deserve love and care and having their needs met, so do you. I know—maybe no one else is treating you that way. Well, that is probably both their self-centeredness and the reality that you've built all the relationships around you so that you are the self-sacrificial caregiver. As a consequence, you may not even be in touch with your needs. This can change. It may be—probably will be—painful for all as that transition happens, but it needs to happen for everyone's good.

Do you think it's really helping others if they are constantly receiving from you and not giving? Nope. We all need the balance of *give* and *receive*. Take it from me. I always felt I had to have the caretaker role in my family so that people survived and had what they needed. It's likely that was true at certain times. Gone unmoderated, it made me start to think that others can't function without me, I don't have an identity if I'm not the caretaker, or kept me from allowing others the room they need to grow, make mistakes, and take care of themselves.

You are so worth taking care of. Only the devil would create a lie that says otherwise. Hopefully, you know the Church does not condone the well-meant but not fully informed forms of self-mortification the saints practiced of old. Understanding these things grows over time.

We spend a lot of time trying to alleviate sufferings—whether physical, mental, or emotional—but then we sometimes also feel like we need to create sufferings for ourselves to be more holy... Nope. In fact, as St. Paul writes, the path of holiness lies much more in being able to accept as best we can the good and bad that come our way naturally. Don't worry, both will come on their own. And it's that path that brings your unique holiness.

Part of your path may be accepting a gluten and dairy-free diet, taking certain prescriptions for physical or mental health, and creating a discipline to work out more regularly. I know, it sounds like a year-round Lent. But there you go—the self-sacrifice is already built in as you try to do life well. No need to sacrifice the identity and physicality God so passionately created for you in order to please him. How much more it pleases him when you take great care of those priceless gifts!

JODY

What does it mean to me to be healthy and practice consistent self-care? It wasn't until I started grad school that I considered self-care. I used to feel guilty for needing any kind of self-care, so I would just plow through life. I was a very active child and enjoyed playing outside all the time. Okay, playing outside looks different as an adult, but I still enjoy my time outdoors.

Growing up watching my mother struggle with weight cultivated an inner vow that drove me to be overactive and healthy. It was also a way for me to relieve my stress from events in my childhood. For thirty-one years, I enjoyed working out and never had an injury until I turned forty-five years old. This devastating event happened at the wrong time. I learned a lot about how emotionally mistuned I was to myself. I'll explain.

Over time, working out stresses the body to the point that you feel sore most of the time. I realized that working out, although a good thing, can be a way to numb your emotions. Attunement to yourself means one ought to be able to feel their bodily sensations and feelings. This is important, because our sensations inform us of the world, which helps us to survive and make decisions.

Being in a constant state of tension meant I was on guard, defenses ready, unable to fully relax. I was chronically in fight mode—my nervous system on overdrive from earlier trauma. This is how my body decided to store the unprocessed trauma. I didn't feel anxious or depressed. I was tense and hypervigilant about my survival. In the world of counseling, we call this survival mode.

My neck injury was the way God was going to help me work through the trauma, restore my attunement, and find balance. Let me explain why attunement is important. It goes back to how we attach to others, God, and ourselves. This will allow us to practice self-care in a healthy way. Self-attunement is the practice of being in tune with your own thoughts, feelings (our bodily sensations provide us the road map to our feelings), and needs. It plays a crucial role in emotional awareness, helping you recognize and manage your emotions effectively. This self-awareness can lead to improved relationships as you can communicate your needs and boundaries more clearly.

Additionally, it aids in stress reduction by allowing you to identify and address stressors proactively. Self-attunement also fosters personal growth through introspection and self-reflection, enhancing decision-making by aligning choices with your values and goals. Ultimately, it supports mental and spiritual health by helping you detect early signs of issues and seek guidance and interventions.

Healthy living and self-care intertwine deeply with spiritual well-being. The Catholic Church teaches that our bodies are temples of the Holy Spirit, and thus, we have a responsibility to care for them. This care extends beyond physical health to include mental, emotional, and spiritual health. Self-care is the balance in all three areas. Most people think self-care is taking care of the physical. Yet, we are created as a body-soul unity—therefore, we can't separate our body from the mental or spiritual aspects of ourselves.

Our society has done a good job at dividing our body from everything else, especially when it comes to sex. Our defenses cut us off from the bodily sensations to dismiss or ignore negative feelings/emotions when they start to bubble up. The effects are devastating. The level of intimacy is limited, and understanding our needs goes unseen. We place ourselves in a perpetual state of emptiness, which leads to loneliness and isolation. God doesn't want that for us.

As Catholics, we are encouraged to eat nutritious foods, exercise regularly, and get adequate rest. These practices not only enhance physical well-being but also provide the energy and vitality needed to serve others and fulfill one's vocation. The Church also emphasizes the importance of moderation and avoiding excess, as gluttony and sloth are considered sins that can harm both body and soul.

Spiritual health is at the core of our self-care. Consistently going to Mass, confession, and engaging in prayer are fundamental practices that nourish the soul. I believe that a strong spiritual life helps us stay connected to God, find meaning and purpose, and navigate life's challenges with grace and resilience. Spiritual direction and retreats are also recommended for deeper reflection and growth.

The Lord showed me what self-care and healthy living mean. Through our trials, He will undo and address the areas of our hearts we never knew needed attention. Give the Lord a chance to show you where to go in your health, self-care, and healing. The goal is to flourish as the best version of yourself in truth, humility, and love.

Side note: My passion for healthy living and self-care carries over to all my relationships. It's very important that my future spouse will find this balance. I want him around for a long time and hope that we will enjoy living a holy and healthy life. God willing!!!

THE CONVERSATION CONTINUES

Soon after I came home from my time in consecrated life (when my cycles stopped and I lost a lot of weight), my parents wanted me to get good medical care, so my mom and I went to go visit the doctors at the University of Michigan, Ann Arbor. They decided to look at my bone density after learning that I was still without a cycle. Little did I know how important estrogen is! At twenty-one, I was diagnosed with severe osteopenia/borderline osteoporosis—they said that my bone density was that of a seventy-five-year-old woman!

Because they wanted me to start receiving estrogen immediately, they put me on a medicine that was the equivalent of birth control. This medicine was a pill I took faithfully for the next five years or so until my engagement to Shannon. His sister is a master herbologist, and when she found out the medicine I had been feeding my body for so long, she told me to immediately stop and take three herbs in particular: dong quai, chasteberry, and a third that neither she nor I can remember!

These three herbs, I personally believe, helped rid my body of the toxins that had built up over those years and possibly prevented any future breast cancer. (Right after starting on this herbal regimen, my chest broke out in a severe rash that lasted for over a week! It was definitely a bit funny on the timing, though, since we had only a few months until the wedding.)

Fast-forward ten years later, and a good friend in our homeschool group, Tracy, shared with me that she also was given the same medicine for the purpose of regulating her cycles. At that point, she had breast cancer and was a few years into regular chemo treatments. She passed away maybe a year or two later, a real saint who was so in love with God and a wonderful/sacrificial mom. She was my exact age and had taken the same pill for the same number of years as I had, until her wedding day when she personally decided to stop and let God take over. St. Tracy, pray for us!

Additionally, during my time at Wayne State, I was asked to join the cross country team. I was considered "old" by the others on the team, being a twenty-four-year-old! Getting to know the other girls on the team, though, showed me how overly prescribed this birth control medicine was at the time: more than half of those young girls (eighteen to twenty years old for the most part) were on birth control—some for their acne, others for irregular periods. What an injustice the medical world was giving to these young and trusting girls!

I experienced gradual healing and my cycle return just by being a mom to my oldest child, Victoria, whom we adopted! It was another five years, though, until my cycle returned once again. I'm not sure exactly what helped bring the sudden overflowing cascade that came on Divine Mercy Sunday and lasted all week in the year of 2014, but for the next four months, I experienced a monthly cycle for the first time in my entire life! That was the year I turned 40.

Looking at different reasons for why I finally experienced full health at this later age, I can give only some thoughts. My mom, for example, would always call me, "a bear for punishment" since I found my fulfillment in long miles, both running and biking. Being a mom tempered those miles by a lot . . . and that didn't happen overnight. It was a gradual transformation from an individual who lived for endorphin highs to a mom who was experiencing a growing love in my heart for these beautiful children in front of me.

Shannon's recipe for my return to health over the years always seemed to be something like this: eat more, sleep more, exercise less. Seriously, though, everyone is completely different! Some women can train for marathons or bike centuries and never lose their monthly cycle, while others risk going overboard by running 10Ks. Maybe the difference lies in the difference in lean muscle and your body fat percentage? There is the right amount . . . going under *or* over that proper range, and achieving a desired pregnancy will be more difficult. Of course, there are other causes and helps, but I think with me, I just gradually became more moderate in my lifestyle . . . due to already living as a mom and the needs of my awesome children right in front of me!

After those incredible four months of living through regular monthly cycles, for the first time in my life, a second pregnancy was confirmed. The following day, I turned forty!

Katherine W.

My number one rule about healthy living is - don't expect to do something 100% of the time or you'll be setting yourself up for stress and disappointment. Many people, out of necessity, commit to healthy practices 100% of the time, but for other healthy lifestyle choices, 75% of the time is good. More than that is great!

My biggest health suggestion is to check out fasting. Eating healthy has two parts . . . what to eat and when to eat it. Most people, advertisements, and stores only focus on what to eat. Fasting is an age-old weight loss and body maintenance practice. Our body has whole processes in place for times of fasting. It's fascinating! Fasting is cheap, simple, and suggested by God to be combined with prayer to make us holier. It makes sense that something God suggested would be good for us in more ways than one.

The other healthy living tip I have is to incorporate natural movements throughout the day. These movements aren't necessarily for exercise but to keep our bodies moving in varied ways well into old age. Here are some examples. Our ancestors squatted . . . a lot. Even ten minutes of squats during exercise isn't much compared to squatting as a way of life. Throw a bolster on the floor and squat to get down and up off that bolster and bam, you can get a lot of squatting in throughout the day. Wearing minimalist shoes or going barefoot are great ways to allow your feet and toes to move as they should. Once you free your toes, they'll never want to go back to traditional shoes again! Touching the door frame as you pass through is a way to get your arms all the way up instead of always being in the front "typing" position. Katy Bowman and Petra Fisher are two movement gurus with lots of resources.

Angela W.

Oh dear, there we go again. Healthy living: I shouldn't eat sweets, I shouldn't eat carbohydrates, I shouldn't sit the whole day . . . healthy living is a big topic today, with good reason, but I think we often associate it with everything I can't do or enjoy. I had to turn that around: how can I take good care of myself so that I feel energetic, so that I take good care of my God-given temple (I had to pray into this one), and so that I can take better care of my husband and the people around me?

Other people will have many opinions: "Don't fuss about it," "Just go running more often," "If you do this, then you will feel great." These suggestions are well meaning, but you are you, and only *you* can take *responsibility* to take good care of yourself! And only you can discover what really works for you: running works for some, not for all; eating sauerkraut works for some, not for all; going cold water swimming works for some (my seventy-year-old parents do that, impressive!), but not for all (not for me—*wink*).

Of course, there are some things which are good for everyone, but I think we know which ones those are. I have learned two things about health over these past years:

1) *Feel* what your body needs. Don't just *think* but really feel. Tune in to your body, your breath . . . I started discovering that when I crave chocolate, it's not always that I need chocolate. Sometimes, I need to talk to my husband, ask for a hug, take a siesta or a bath, eat a banana, or, indeed, eat a piece of chocolate. So, *feel*.

2) Instead of asking, "What is supposed to be good for me now at this moment?" (I got really frustrated, because one health coach/website says A and the other B, and both ended up not being helpful for me), ask, "What *nourishes* me?"

Take your health seriously. You are your body, and you have the responsibility to take care of it. And, sister, you do not need to do this alone! It has helped me so much to receive help from trusted friends and counselors. Do not be ashamed to reach out to someone with any kind of health issues/questions/difficulties. We all have them one way or another.

Chiara D.

Before I was a married woman, and before I was Catholic, for that matter, I was always motivated to lead a "healthy" lifestyle. I ate real food, strived for a balanced diet, and went to the gym . . . well, I usually went to the gym. Now, I realize healthy living encompasses so much more for my family. Not only are we eating well and physically active, but we're maintaining healthy relationships, maintaining healthy moods (in a house with four girls), and maintaining a healthy and Godly respect for ourselves and our bodies!

It can be daunting to make changes and progress, but we've found that taking small steps and making goals works best for us. We strive to see friends at least once a week, pray daily as a family, limit eating out, and go to the gym. Most importantly, if we notice the family becoming overwhelmed, we slow down and make sure our prayer life is healthy. We aren't perfect, and an aspect or two of our healthy lifestyle is sometimes lacking (mostly the gym), but with prayer and persistence, we can always get back on track.

Courtney B.

CHAPTER ELEVEN

God and the Catholic Church

She opens her mouth in wisdom;
kindly instruction is on her tongue.

She watches over the affairs of her household,
and does not eat the bread of idleness.

PROVERBS 31:26–27

Simon Peter answered him, "Master, to whom shall we go? You have the words of eternal life. We have come to believe and are convinced that you are the Holy One of God."

JOHN 6:68–69

MARNEE

I am fortunate that I grew up in a little area that was very Catholic. My parents were both Catholic, and I received all the sacraments and participated in many Catholic extracurriculars. I came of age during the time of a thriving Catholic youth group, the expansion of Steubenville Youth Conferences, and the growing popularity of "Come and See" retreats for religious orders.

I've attended talks by many of the prominent Catholic speakers of the day and got my bachelor of theology from a local seminary. I've been to Rome a couple times and to Medjugorje, and I have lived in Argentina doing mission work with religious sisters. I have a couple of brothers who discerned the priesthood and a sister who is now a cloistered nun. All in all, a life filled with much Catholicity!

My Catholic faith is integrally a part of me, and I wouldn't trade it or change it. The root of it, of course, is my relationship with God. As one of my sisters said, "It's not about the people" (or the politics or the places), and it never could be. Only God has the "words of eternal life."

My relationship with God has had its trials, though. That quote above about "where else would we go" . . . Yeah, there have been those moments, hanging on by sheer willpower (with an essential dose of humility). There is a line in the movie *The Painted Veil* where a seasoned missionary nun says her relationship with God has become a very comfortable and familiar one: "He knows I will never leave him," she says. And that is relatable, too.

The journey to a balanced and solid faith integration has been a long and complex one. As a mental health counselor, I see most of my Catholic clients wrestling through it as well. Some of these old and flawed perceptions are amazingly still passed around and embedded into our psyches. Ideas like God being the disapproving judge—punitive, perfectionistic, shaming. When I went through an extended healing prayer session a while back, I found myself coming up against wave after wave of cold, distant, God figures. Statues, masks, all disinterested and condemning.

When that is our God, we are never enough. We may be driven to scrupulosity (a religious manifestation of obsessive-compulsive disorder), trying to earn our way into heaven. We have no mercy on ourselves because we don't expect God will have mercy on us. We have the odd notion that too much mercy is weak and liberal . . . ha!

So, we can find ourselves falling into OCD-type spiritual patterns: Did we say that Hail Mary with perfect fervor? (No? Say it again, and again!) Did we miss a weekday Mass when we just resolved to have 100% attendance? Did we accidentally eat meat on a Friday in Lent? Did we not say that thing to that person that we thought maybe we should, and now their salvation may be lost? These thoughts can pile up and plague us into either despair or unyielding motion. We find peace in neither, but our salvation feels like it hangs in the balance, and so trying another approach is too terrifying to consider.

As with so many spiritual realities, what lies on the other side of that seemingly impenetrable wall of fear is not death but freedom. God offers freedom. Peace. A love that will do anything for you. If those sound like foreign concepts (or you think they are meant for others, not you—a "great sinner"), then likely God is calling you to make a giant, freeing leap of faith into his arms.

It's important to remember that there are two hallmarks of spiritual OCD or scrupulosity. One, we consider ourselves supremely unique in how God is telling us to do these obsessive and penitential things, and therefore, any advice offered by others is rejected as "not understanding." (We can see here that what seems like humility is really pride.) The other is a debilitating fear of damnation. Every little error seems to ensure our loss of heaven. Therefore, we are too terrified to change our behavior or risk mistakes, as the stakes seem to be all or nothing. That is not God.

Speaking of the Church, I'd like to warn about the danger of putting religious leaders or influencers on pedestals. Let's face it; our religious leaders wield a lot of power, so it can be tempting for them and for us to revere them a bit too much, hang on their every word, especially if said authority figure seems to thrive in creating a personality cult around themselves.

These situations usually breed disillusionment when that figure inevitably falls, but in the meantime, they can also shift a person's focus away from God himself. When I was reflecting on this recently, it made me think of when Jesus says call no man father. The way I hear it, he is essentially warning us not to put anyone except God himself into that position of authority in our lives—the position of father and child, the most powerful relationship of master/teacher/model.

It sure is hard to be Catholic sometimes! I remember being interviewed by a local news station several years ago in the wake of priest abuses, and that was one of the lines they quoted me directly on, omitting the line that followed, "but it's worth it!" People laugh at us, look down on us, try to shake or confuse us, get irritated, put on pressure, or simply shake their heads and walk away. It can be hard to withstand. We each have our shame triggers and don't handle it well when they get pushed. But we really can't be surprised; Jesus has been telling us to expect it for 2,000 years. *Insert brunette shrugging emoji.*

Sometimes, it doesn't look like there's too much difference

between Christians and non-Christians in terms of prosperity or happiness or getting what you want in the world. But there are a few deeper differences that I'm guessing you've noticed.

1. Peace. When God says he gives us "the peace the world cannot give," he's right on.
2. Faith. Hard times come for everyone. You notice how people handle it. There's a difference.
3. Hope. Hard times come for everyone. You notice how people respond. Their outlook on life is different.
4. Love. Okay, I did not intend to write these three; they just individually came to mind. What can I say? Love is a complex word today, but let's think of it in terms of self-sacrifice, orientation towards others, long suffering, etc. There is a big difference in depth here.
5. Suffering. We all have it. Sometimes, it's unbearable. But we bear it. No, I'm not going to say "offer it up" (a triggered phrase for many of us . . .). I'm going to say, it's already offered up. God knows. He's a heart-reader. Christians definitely wear this one differently. We may not have the answer, but we know suffering doesn't get the final word.

In the opening pages of this book, we describe ourselves (the writers) as Catholic women who love our faith, and when we have concerns or doubts, we trust, learn, pray, and have patience. We know God is here in this faith, but we also know it doesn't give us a step-by-step guidebook for living. If you find yourself trying your best, being humble, and seeking guidance, but still not seeing that God manifestation explicitly telling you what to do, I think it means he trusts you to rely on the resources he is sending your way. He is not a perfectionist and is not waiting for you to trip up over insight you don't have. He doesn't play mind games. He's not manipulative. Those are fallen human traits.

This faith is often not easy to live, but I do believe it has the words of eternal life, and there is no question it's worth it to be here.

JODY

Where do I begin? Faith is a grace that I received through no merits of my own. I was baptized at four years old, went to a Catholic school for about three and half years, attended religious education for one year, yet I did not practice the faith in the home, ever. The little exposure I had to the Catholic Church was enough for me to know I would one day get confirmed.

I remember a friend in high school who was Christian but not Catholic inviting me to her young adult Bible study on Wednesday nights. They would take time to pray with each other and offer up intentions. Yes, they prayed out loud! This was so new to me, but I sat there in awe. However, as they were praying, I would be saying Hail Marys. The Catholic faith never left me, even if I wasn't practicing. Mind you, I didn't go there instead of the Catholic Church; it was a way for me to escape being at home, and I got to spend time with a good friend.

When I turned twenty-two years old, my mother-in-law would go to church. I asked if I could join her, and with such gentleness, she said, "Of course you can." After a while, my husband joined, and we went every Sunday.

I started Rite of Christian Initiation of Adults (RCIA), and at the age of twenty-four, I was confirmed into the Church. That day was life-changing. I have not been the same since. From that point on, my faith life has been exponentially growing with moments of big leaps forward. The biggest leap was when I worked at the pregnancy care center. I prayed for God to send me friends that would help me grow in my faith, and boy did he. They were a group of women who really lived out their faith and knew a lot. I had a voracious appetite to learn as much about the faith as possible. There was so much I didn't know and still don't.

It's funny what God uses to nudge us closer to him. In my early thirties, I started to get involved in current events and politics but had a desire to go deeper into my faith. During that time, I was learning about American history and our founding fathers. I realized what they shared in common and how they constructed America based on Christian values.

I started studying more American history, which led me to the Bible. It took me about three years to read it from cover to cover. Then I turned to Catholic Church history. God knew my love for history and placed the breadcrumbs that would lead me to a deeper relationship with him. It's beautiful how he got my attention. Take a moment and ponder how God led you to the Church or to go deeper in your faith. Where are the breadcrumbs leading you currently?

I was exposed to other denominations a few times, but they never filled my cup or felt right to me. The Catholic Church offers explanations for my suffering, purpose, vocation, and the importance of being united with Christ through the Eucharist. This is where I learned about my femininity and created design. Everything the Church offers is ordered towards my ultimate good and flourishing. And I have to agree with Marnee that it is dang hard to be Catholic!! Although I wouldn't change it, there are days where I can see why St. Teresa of Avila said, "If this is how you treat your friends, no wonder you have so few!"

My relationship with Christ over the past ten years has been all over the place. Moments of gratitude, then questioning his love for me, then not wanting to have anything to do with him, then feeling bad I yelled at him after he blessed me, and then coming to a place of some understanding. He has been teaching me what it is like to be in a healthy relationship.

I talk about secure attachment throughout this book. Overall, the Catholic Church provides a safe, supportive, and nurturing environment (though I understand it is not perfect, and there are those who were hurt by a clergy or staff member). It gives me a way to come to Christ in a real way (physically, emotionally, spiritually). During these ten years, I focused on my healing while he focused on our relationship. I learned I had more of an anxious attachment style to God. We project our attachment style that we developed with our parents onto God.

Let me explain.

A secure parent is responsive, emotionally available, consistent, upholds healthy boundaries, encourages exploration, and gives positive reinforcement more often than not. They are very consistent with their care. If, for whatever reason, a parent isn't capable of providing this care consistently, the child will develop an unhealthy attachment style. There are three: anxious, avoidant, and disorganized (a combo of anxious and avoidant).

Okay, so what does this all mean, Jody? Get to the point!

The point is that attachment styles can significantly influence how individuals perceive and relate to God. Those with a secure attachment style often view God as a reliable and loving presence, feeling comfortable in their faith and spiritual practices. Individuals with an anxious attachment style may seek constant reassurance from their relationship with God, often worrying about their worthiness or God's responsiveness. Those with an avoidant attachment style might struggle with intimacy in their spiritual life, keeping a distance from religious practices or viewing God as distant. Lastly, individuals with a disorganized attachment style may have a conflicted or inconsistent relationship with God, reflecting their past experiences of trauma or inconsistent caregiving. Understanding these dynamics can help individuals navigate their spiritual journey and foster a healthier, more fulfilling relationship with God.

Next, I want to mention the current state of the Church. The Church has gone through many popes, changes, and divisions. Jesus encountered a similar situation with the Pharisees. He gave us an example of how to handle matters like this. He challenged their hearts and behavior to help guide them back to the Father. He also honored their free will.

St. Bernadette Soubirous said, "I am here to inform, not to convince." I think it would be prudent to take this advice when struggling with the heated issues at hand. Bring everything you do to prayer. Be silent until instructed to speak. God will use those who are given those graces to address the matters, and he will instruct others to do their part. Let's have confidence in how the Lord will guide us through these events.

I am referring mostly to the tensions between different factions in Catholicism. Let's remember that we are all united under the Universal Church. My relationship with God will be different than yours or any other person's. Let's support one another and agree to live a life in truth. God will sort out all the details.

My loyalties are not with certain people in the Church; they are with God and the Magisterium. Therefore, my desire is to follow the most theologically sound path God has provided. Let's be disciples of Christ and practice the virtues of faith, hope, and charity and try to have some fun being daughters of God.

Finally, my faith is what drives me in everything I do. It's my worldview and the way I live. During my darkest days, it was my faith that sustained me. How, you ask? By graces. The graces of hope, resiliency, and purpose. My church family gave me the love and support I needed when I had nothing left, when I felt lost and needed comfort. Where else would I go? The world doesn't provide graces to sustain life, but God does. If you haven't gone to church in a while, I encourage you to go. Give the Lord everything that's on your heart and mind. He can handle it. Just don't give up on him because he will never give up on you.

THE CONVERSATION CONTINUES

Choosing to love the Church has not always been easy. As a young child, I have vivid memories of lying on a pew, my head in my grandmother's lap, and her stroking my hair as she participated in the Mass. I was safe. I was at home. Somewhere along the way, my parents had fallen away from the faith, but in second grade, when I learned that all of my classmates were preparing for their First Communion, I begged to be a part of what everyone else was doing, and my parents returned to the Church. I once again found home.

Over the years, my faith life ebbed and flowed. Sometimes I've been all in, and sometimes I didn't even make it to Mass regularly. But I always knew she was there, anytime I wanted to return. I knew deeply that her laws and traditions were what was best for me. Ultimately, as hard as they can feel sometimes, her laws and traditions lead me closer to him and who he wants me to be.

As I settle into "middle-age," I find so much comfort and consolation in her laws and traditions. I know that my home on earth is only a short stop on my way to my home in heaven. I have become so grateful for the shelter she has provided and the path she has lit for me, especially on some very dark nights. I know that Mother Church always wants what's best for me; always waiting with a smile and arms that are wide open. In her, I have found home.

Chancey M.

In my relationship with the Church, I fell in love with her at the same time I was falling in love with Christ. I realized all of a sudden that she was the Church that Christ himself founded. I realized that she plays such a motherly role for us. She cares about all aspects of our lives. She is ready to guide us, even into uncharted territory! It is one of my deepest sorrows to see people I love reject the Catholic Church.

I think the most consoling statement about this that I have ever heard came from Archbishop Fulton Sheen. He said, "There are not one hundred people in the United States who hate the Catholic Church, but there are millions who hate what they wrongly perceive the Catholic Church to be." I believe that is true. I believe that the fallen-away Catholics have just to rediscover what the Church really is.

Sr. Holy Family

There is an attribute of God that I never hear spoken of . . . He is all good, all loving, all intelligent, all powerful, all knowing—*and* he is all *funny*, full of good humor! When you see others who are gifted with a good sense of humor, remember that their Creator gave them that particular gift! (Any gifts he gives us can be used for what is not good . . . then we are distorting the gifts we've been given, and this applies to humor. We've all seen examples of bad humor—that is not of God!)

My point comes from looking back over the years of raising our children. God has shown so clearly through them that he is truly all funny! (If someone can find a YouTube talk on this topic, please forward it to the rest of us!) Just watching children grow and learn with their completely innocent hearts can lead to the funniest moments in parenting . . . which then allows for a deep, uncontrollable laugh . . . which then makes everyone feel so good. That is definitely from our good God!

Katherine W.

As a child, I had no concept of the fact that Catholicism was not just the default state of belief for everyone. At the same time, I am not sure I had a strong grasp on even what Catholicism was because it was my default. Catholicism was the norm; non-Catholic beliefs were the deviation.

As I began to see more outside of myself, I learned that there were other religions and even different branches of Christianity! This was super confusing. Why does it seem that everyone has slightly different beliefs about every little thing? There are so many opinions, and people just argue and argue.

I have been witnessing this conflict in the people around me and in myself my whole life, especially since I began attending a public university and spent two years in the Army. This conflict instilled fear in my heart: What if I lost myself amidst the noise?

Everyone is trying to grasp their own kind of truth in their own type of way, and it's very convoluted. To address the fear, I began to seek out what the Catholic Church actually stood for. I was delighted to find that it was literally a rock amidst the relativism and progressivism in my daily life. It is so incredibly beautiful and has been a testament of strength for over 2,000 years! Wherever in the world I find myself, a Catholic Church always feels a bit like home, even when everything else is foreign to me.

Mary-Elizabeth W.

CHAPTER TWELVE

Flourishing

She is clothed with strength and dignity,
and laughs at the days to come.

PROVERBS 31:25

For the fruit of noble struggles is a glorious one;
and unfailing is the root of understanding.

WISDOM 3:15

MARNEE

This earth is not heaven, though it may have some heaven-like moments. For my perfectionist and idealistic mind, I need to remember that mishaps, struggles, and imperfections are part of the human experience here on earth. They will not be solved or gotten rid of in our lifetime (though we do have so many means of making our lives easier). To expect them to go away at some point breeds frustration and discouragement. No, these challenges are not the exception—the moments of pure goodness and joy are. How wonderful it will be to be in heaven! An idealist, perfectionist, romantic's dream! I already told my husband I plan to spend the first 100,000 years just walking and holding his hand.

However, one of God's great and mysterious abilities is bringing goodness out of evil, bringing joy and hope into the darkest experiences, and blessing our lives with peace and providence when we strive after him. In fact, he desires each of us to have a full and happy life. Flourishing isn't a "happily ever after," but it is a meaningful life lived according to who God designed you to be—full of contentment, passion, purpose, and reward.

To me, flourishing is a deep place. I remember a confession once where the priest talked about a deep interior stillness or peace, like the depths of the ocean, even when storms are raging on the surface of life. I don't think I had that deep peacefulness for a long time, but I could still imagine the concept.

I have an experience of this peace now. It seems to me that being in that place is a key component of flourishing. Maybe because it's not achievable if we're not in touch with and accepting of who we truly are in God's eyes. That requires lots of honesty, humility, love, and patience, among other things.

Flourishing carries a sense of happiness with it, too. It is a positive experience to flourish and it sounds delightful. But it's one of those words that goes beyond the superficial. A flourishing plant has good roots, enough nurturing, the right amount of sun. In this nourishing environment, the plant becomes healthy, strong, and vibrant, which gives life to others out of an abundance of the full life it has in itself. Those types of experiences all point clearly to God. A God who designs, cultivates, nourishes, and cherishes his creation.

Flourishing is not synonymous with easy. Or lucky. Or even success - Though there may be those moments. Flourishing takes continual effort, sacrifice, digging deep . . . and brings profound reward.

I find this a challenging concept overall. It seems like many of the deepest realities are hardest to explain or understand, but you know them when you feel them or when you see them. Maybe flourishing was that quality that pagans recognized in the early Christians even as they lived under continual persecution and faced terrible deaths. Maybe flourishing comes out of love of God and neighbor. Probably. I think I included this chapter, as abstract as it is, because it points to a core aspect of the Christian life that warrants more discussion.

You cannot define flourishing by external signs. External circumstances will not affect it. I think at its core, when a person flourishes, it is not something that is flaunted or grasped at, because, in essence, it is undeniably a gift. When something is a gift (both undeserved yet also gained through very intentional living), it doesn't come from you. So, you feel no right to boast in it.

Painfully, that also means you cannot gift it to others. For someone who experiences it, you want nothing more than to give it to everyone you know. You wish it for them so much— particularly those who are suffering. Yet, it's not yours to give; it's a choice of life each has to make for themselves.

Here are some ways of living that seem to lead towards flourishing:

- Working consistently on self-awareness and using that humble knowledge to foster greater empathy towards others
- Finding hidden ways to serve those around you in love and joy
- Giving generously to others as you are able
- Taking time for silent prayer, conversation, reflection, or simply being with God
- Affirming someone else in their goodness, beauty, or talents
- Sitting back and really listening to others
- Reveling in the beauty of creation
- Fostering a child-like sense of wonder
- Reflecting on gratitude and hopefulness
- Surrendering your preference for someone else's preference sometimes
- Taking extra steps towards establishing personal connections
- Doing good things you thrive at

If you find people who seem to be flourishing contentedly in their (often quiet) lives, take note of where their values and priorities lie. Talk to them about what brings them fulfillment. Share your own experiences of what has brought peace and meaning to your life and what has detracted from it.

It is essential to be aware of the world outside of our own minds. Authentic truth-seekers will find truth. I agree with the spirit of Pope Francis's message that there is no need to be afraid of all the many opinions and ideas surrounding us. I believe a heart set on truth will not be deceived for long. So much that is hammering us from the world, with all its bravado, is merely "a resounding gong and clashing cymbal" or "vanity" as Scripture says. It is empty and shallow, which we know in our honesty.

We do not hold the fullness of truth within the limits of our minds. We must spend our lifetime being open to growing in that truth through encounters and revelations we receive along the way. Truth will set us free. Truth about ourselves, God, others, and the meaning of life will lead us to flourishing. If we kindle these desires in ourselves, like a candle at an Easter Vigil Mass, it will slowly but surely share its fire with others. But that is not ultimately our responsibility.

As confused and disordered as many things are in the world today, God does not have generalized anxiety disorder as a result. Neither does he have major depressive disorder or OCD. Meaning, yes, he carries the *weight of the world* and *loves it beyond imagining*. He also intervenes at every opportunity and makes every effort to bring good from bad. He feels and knows and does so much more than we ever could! But he is not changed by the evil that exists, nor is he burdened by it. His self is unwavering and unchanging.

Likewise, I think we are called to live that way. We love, we help, we pray, but we do not worry. Today's troubles are enough for today. And our own salvation is the only one we are ultimately in control of. If we say our yesses, others will be more likely to say theirs, too. And we will certainly rejoice with them when we are flourishing together.

However, if we get entangled with the darkness around us to such an extent that we lose our light or we begin to confuse what is up and what is down, we do no one any good. Playing with the darkness does not create more light. Carrying the weight of the world on our shoulders crushes us. Is it not more humble and realistic to cast that burden on God, whose shoulders are made for it, and simply seek the ways we can be a part of his plan? Our own self-sized role, a perfect fit, a fulfilling calling, is found only in the perspective of ourselves in relationship to God.

One final thought on flourishing. The gospel reading I heard today was from Luke 5, the miraculous catch of fish. When the Lord calls someone to do a work, the abundance that follows is so clearly from his hand. It struck Peter to an awe that was almost terror because there was no question his labor yielded fruitfulness beyond his efforts.

When we stand before those kinds of results, they bring us to profound humility instead of pride, just as Peter went immediately to kneel at the feet of Jesus. That is another way to identify the Lord's work in our lives. I have witnessed it in the process of writing this book, in the work my husband and I do, and in many relationships. Letting the Lord in can mean abdicating some level of control or expectation, but it always ends up giving us what we most desire to the point that our "cup runneth over."

JODY

I think we all want to flourish. Yet, we might all have a different definition. It's important to note that flourishing is not happiness. We can feel happy when we are flourishing, an acknowledgement that we are balanced and have a good enough understanding of our personhood.

I have thought about what flourishing means to me many times, especially during times of suffering or moments of feeling lost. I look back at the varied expectations when I was younger. After living some years now, I've realized that flourishing isn't a stagnant state of being. God willing, we are ever changing, maturing, and being refined into the best version of ourselves that God created.

One may have an image of what they think their best version is. You know, the "ideal" self. "I am woman, hear me roar!" I have it all together, I can manage the messiness of life while maintaining emotional and physical awesomeness, being there for everyone, taking care of all my needs, never wanting for anything, working forty hours, keeping my house in order, and practicing self-care by superficial self-sacrifice.

Hmmm, that doesn't seem sustainable or realistic, and yet a lot of women have some version of this they are striving for. I did, to some extent. It's because we are uncomfortable with our own dignity and worth. Think about it. How do you respond to a compliment, self-care (what we discussed in the earlier chapter), or when others see, value, and hear *you*, without you doing anything for them? (Take a pause here and breathe. Give yourself a moment to sit with these questions).

We hear how we are created in his likeness and image. What does that mean for me? It means that I scrap the "ideal" self (from the distorted view of self usually developed out of woundedness and negative beliefs about oneself) and allow God to transfigure me without limitations. Because I have the image and likeness of God, I have the ability to reason, exercise free will, and love selflessly.

I can love selflessly by living the Beatitudes, practicing virtues, embracing my unique qualities, and accepting *all* of myself. Yes, *all* of yourself. Your positive *and* negative aspects matter. Your dignity doesn't have to be earned or dependent on any external factors such as achievements, abilities, wealth, or if you stay at home or if you work. You don't have to jump through hoops for God to see you. He delights in you.

Flourishing isn't looking for ways for you to be "fixed" or perceiving you as "the problem." You are distracting yourself from accepting *all* of you. Stop "fixing" yourself so you can allow God to transform you. Please stop reducing your dignity to the things you find "wrong" with you. Trust God that he can work with all your flaws, problems, and imperfections.

If you are not convinced, then look at all the people in the Bible: Moses, David, Peter, Paul, etc. Flourishing is building off your strengths and embracing everything else. A life of chasing the "if only" or "it's not good enough" attitude in everything will keep you in the self-loathing loop. The enemy will use that to distract you from God and distort how you see yourself, which robs you from flourishing.

My sisters in Christ, it's okay to love the person God created in you. You don't have to do very much—just give him your heart (fifteen minutes a day to be still in your worth with Jesus, don't bring anything to read, no rosary, or ear pods . . .) and the opportunity to reclaim you as his (ask to see yourself through his eyes). This is where you will be able to receive his love and see yourself truly for the first time.

Look out!! You might like what you see and fall in love with his creation through you.

I understand this is all easier said than done. It will take time. Embrace the process. There is so much he wants to give you along the path to flourishing.

THE CONVERSATION CONTINUES

I love the name of this chapter: "Flourishing." It reminds me of the flowery print that is in style now. I see an overabundant tomato plant. Life. Fruitfulness. Unhindered growth. It brings to my mind one of my all-time favorite quotes that I find myself writing time and time again in my "book of consolation" (which is a pretty notebook I keep full of encouraging and thought-provoking citations from Scripture and spiritual reading). It can be found in the *Catechism of the Catholic Church* number 294: "The glory of God is man fully alive," Saint Irenaeus.

God is glorified when we flourish. So, flourish! Don't be afraid to grow and let yourself be nurtured! I think some Catholics get their wires crossed, thinking that God wants us to find things to suffer and crosses to pick up to keep us down and out. Nothing could be farther from the truth. When Christ carried his cross, he did it freely and with ardent, burning love. Flourishing doesn't mean "everything is easy" but that "everything works for the good of those who love God" (Romans 8:28).

Sr. Holy Family

I want to stress again the deep impression left on my whole being when I was told to go home (from consecrated life) and get healthy: God *loves me*! This conviction has carried me through marriage and family life, along with the daily grace of his sacraments. Without it, marriage and family life would be impossible.

In the dark, painful, ugly moments that life has brought in these last twenty-two years of married and family life . . . in those moments that my prayer has been almost wordless—just an act of trust that God sees me, he sees this—he loves me and will carry us through this moment. He made us for union with him in heaven . . . and union with each other there as well. He wants us in heaven with him more than we want it; so this trust in his *love* for *me* has been such a gift.

To be a bit more honest, though, the gift of endorphins has also been a huge help! Maybe it was the time of running at Wayne State, but sometime in the past, I developed a severe addiction to endorphins, for which I am also very grateful! It's been in those long bike rides, walks, and swims that the best reflections and prayers have been made! And those "feel-good" endorphins have given the added push needed for daily perseverance! Biking, swimming, and walking have also been a great way to bond with my kids and help them a bit where they may need healing.

Katherine W.

You and I are made as the crown of creation, to show the beauty of God in this world! Oh, how I wish for all of us that we realize this in our daily lives. Our longings and talents are put in us by God, whether that is a talent of, or having the longing for, being a mother, doctor, lawyer, painter, musician, housewife, animal trainer, or mountaineer. . . . I have experienced that when I go deep in my heart, through taking time for journaling, I discover what my deepest longings are: to flourish, to be free of what holds me back, and to help other women to flourish.

By discovering what holds me back, I have been able to overcome it. Some of my fears: expectations of others and myself; me not trusting God and not daring to "jump;" the fear of what others might say or think. Oh boy, but when I let go of these fears, through prayer, journaling, and talking with others, I feel so free! I start dancing to music, I start actually following my heart's desires, and there is space for my God-given talents to flourish! Yes, it is hard work, but oh, women, it is so worthwhile!

Chiara D.

I always like to begin with a little research. The first definition of the verb to flourish found in the online version of the *Merriam-Webster Dictionary* means to grow luxuriantly; to thrive. Luxuriantly is a delightful adverb, indicating not simply luxury but rather (and more excellently) a manner of acting that yields abundant fruit.

Knowing now what we aim for, i.e., what it means to flourish, I wander into new questions: For what sort of flourishing should I aim for, why should I flourish, and how do I do that?

Each woman flourishes differently and perhaps even for different reasons. Yet, reflecting on my own journey—one that is akin to a rollercoaster that can defy the laws of physics and sometimes leaves you whiplashed—I recognized two truths: (1) those who fail to flourish set the bar too low and fail to risk; and (2) flourishing is a lifelong endeavor with an uneven trajectory of growth that requires faith, hope, trust, and perseverance.

To grow luxuriantly . . . how often I have grasped for security—whether monetary or simply a security rooted in other people's good opinions of me! (It's far more often than I care to admit.) Yet, this default definition of flourishing or abundant growth limited to human goods (e.g., money, power, esteem, reputation) does not constitute an end in itself. Money, power, and esteem are utilitarian means to some other end. They are too flimsy, too ephemeral to constitute authentic thriving.

True flourishing is much deeper and more elusive. I have found it requires an indefatigable disposition to ask myself the following questions, sometimes daily: Who am I? What is it that I am truly longing for? Why am I here? How can I help others? Perhaps the last question is a partial response to those prior.

After years of striving, I recognized one of my deepest longings is for home and for community. My sense of who I am and the sort of woman I hope to become as I continue my journey is bound up in a sense of community and service to others. And, though it takes a variety of forms, I believe that statement holds true for all women. The natural capacity to grow and bear another person within our own bodies indicates a similar spiritual capacity as well. Flourishing does not end in exterior accomplishments or accolades.

You might imagine that the whole process got easier once I made those discoveries, but in fact, the hardest work was just beginning. I now had to muster the courage to ask the tougher questions: What's getting in the way of me finding home and community? More often than not, the answer to that question was me: my perfectionist tendencies, my rather strong (to put it lightly) choleric streak, my fierce grip on wanting to be right, and all the brokenness I had endured along the journey of life.

The barrier to flourishing was me. And so, I began the slow and lifelong process of healing. It's not always pretty, but there is joy and hope and peace.

And so, the pinnacle of flourishing is the ability to persevere in the pursuit of your deepest longings with sufficient ability to recognize the abundance already present in your life, to rejoice in that abundance, and to allow yourself the time and space to contemplate the beauty of the journey (and, more importantly, the wondrous people you meet and love along the way). The secret to growing luxuriously is, not so simply, the courage to ask the right questions and not to fear the answers, the perseverance to endure the growing pains, the determination to rejoice in the beauty of the present moment, and the capacity to share those experiences with others.

Krystyn S.

Thank you, every woman, for the simple fact of being a woman! Through the insight which is so much a part of your womanhood you enrich the world's understanding and help to make human relations more honest and authentic.

POPE JOHN PAUL II, *LETTER TO WOMEN*

A Woman's Prayer

Dear Lord, you search me, and you know me. I want you to know all, even the dark and shame-filled places. You see my desires and what I have to offer. My abilities and limitations are not lacking or disappointing to you—they are made to serve a great purpose. I have amazing qualities in my design. My beauty has impact. My heart is deep and good. Keep me close to you, and continue to mold and shape my womanly gifts.

Where there are lies, cast them out with truth. Where there are wounds, bind them with your gentle hands in your perfect time. Where there is strength, give me boldness to embrace it. Where there is passion, fan the flame of the desires that you yourself have created for me to live out.

Bring me, Lord, into the vocation you have prepared for me, and may I not lose heart along the way. Bring also into my life many godly women who will support, encourage, teach, and love me into my full womanhood.

Heal all the attachment and relational distortions I was taught when I had to survive. Make me a light on a hilltop for all to see the good God that you are and the incredible vision you have for *woman*. Amen.

Resources

Here are resources recommended by the authors, contributors, or other Catholic mental health professionals. We, the authors, do not vouch for every resource as we have not read them all, but we trust in the benefit others have found. Use your own internal resources to "test everything and retain what is good."

ADHD

Taking Charge of Adult ADHD by Russell Barkley

Smart but Scattered by Peg Dawson and Richard Guare

A Radical Guide for Women with ADHD: Embrace Neurodiversity, Live Boldly, and Break Through Barriers by Sari Solden and Michelle Frank

ALTERNATIVE/SOMATIC HEALING

RestorativeCatholic.com

SoulsandHearts.com

BETRAYAL TRAUMA

BloomForWomen.com

SALifeLine.org

CHILDREN

Beloved Daughter by Carrie Daunt

ElesPlace.org

Here I Am by Abigail Favale

A Terrible Thing Happened by Margaret M. Holmes

Tear Soup: A Recipe for Healing After Loss by Pat Schwiebert and Chuck DeKlyen

COACHING (LIFE, SPIRITUAL, NUTRITION, ETC.)

CatholicLifeCoaches.com

DirectionForYourSoul.com

DOMESTIC ABUSE (PHYSICAL, MENTAL, EMOTIONAL)

Hotline: 800-799-7233

Text BEGIN to 88788

Definition and resources: https://resources.catholicaoc.org/offices/respect-life-ministries/issues/domestic-violence

FASHION

It's So You by Mary Sheehan Warren

Verily.com

FERTILITY/NFP/CYCLE TRACKING

Creightonmodel.com

Marquette.edu

Miracare.com

MMNFP.com

NaturalWomanhood.com

NaturalWomanhood.org/period-genius/ for your daughters

ReplyFertility.com

Unleash the Power of the Female Brain by Daniel Amen

Real Food for Fertility by Lily Nichols and Lisa Hendrickson

The Natural Woman Podcast with Grace Emily Stark

The Language of Your Body by Christina Valenzuela

LOVED ONES WITH MENTAL ILLNESS

Walking on Eggshells by Randi Kreger, Christine Adamec, and Daneil Lobel

MARRIAGE RESOURCES

Ask Christopher West Podcast on Theology and the Body

Love and War by John and Stasi Eldredge

The Seven Principles of Making Marriage Work by John Gottman

HelpYourMarriage.org

HarvilleandHelen.com/couples-workshops/

Created for Connection by Sue Johnson

JPIIHealingCenter.org/unveiled/

OurLadyofBethesda.org/strengthening-your-marriage-communication-workshop

MENTAL WELLNESS

The Emotions God Gave You by Art and Laraine Bennett

I Thought It Was Just Me But It Isn't by Brené Brown

Boundaries (series) by Henry Cloud and John Townsend

Litanies of the Heart by Gerry Ken Crete

The Context of Holiness: Psychological and Spiritual Reflections on the Life of St. Thérèse of Lisieux by Mark Foley

Introduction to the Devout Life by St. Francis de Sales

Life-Giving Love (series) by Kimberly Hahn

Made for This: The Catholic Mom's Guide to Birth by Mary Haseltine

Love As I Am by Sr. Miriam James Heidland

The Presence of God by Ryan Lister

Will I Ever Be Good Enough?: Healing the Daughters of Narcissistic Mothers by Karyl McBride

The Road to Self-Awareness by Ian Murphy

Be Healed by Bob Schuchts

The Intuitive Eating Workbook by Evelyn Tribole and Elyse Resch

The Body Keeps the Score by Bessel van der Kolk

Overcoming Unwanted Intrusive Thoughts by Sally Winston and Martin Seif

PREGNANCY AND LOSS

Nine Months With God and Your Baby: Spiritual Preparation for Birth by Éline Landon

A Catholic Guide to Miscarriage, Stillbirth, and Infant Loss by Abigail Jorgensen

www.RedBird.love

SAME-SEX ATTRACTION

EdenInvitation.com

SCRUPULOSITY

Understanding Scrupulosity by Fr. Thomas Santa

ManagingScrupulosity.com

SEXUAL ADDICTION

MagdalaMinistries.org

SA.org

SURVIVORS OF ABUSE

The Murray Method by Marilyn Murray

Matthew 18: A Conversation Between a Survivor of Child Sexual Abuse and a Catholic Bishop by Carrie Bucalo and Bishop Bill Muhm

THERAPY/PSYCHIATRIC SERVICES

CatholicTherapists.com

DivineMercy.edu > Alumni Directory > M.S in Counseling or Psy. D.

MyCatholicDoctor.com

PsychologyToday.com (you can search for Christian)

WOMEN'S HEALTH

Chiropractic care

Fertilitycare.org (NaProTECHNOLOGY)

Femmhealth.org (medical providers)

Foodallergy.com

Hormone Intelligence by Aviva Romm

MyCatholicDoctor.com

ReformWellness.co

Tests we recommend you request from your health practitioner:

  Thyroid blood panel

  Hormones at respective cycle times

  Vit D and iron levels

WOMEN'S SPIRITUAL GROWTH

AllThingsWomen.org

DirectionForYourSoul.com

DivineMercy.edu > alumni directory > Spiritual Direction Certificate

JPIIHealingCenter.org

Magnificat90.nl (a Dutch site: click translate on the right of the address bar for English)

OLSCretreat.org

www.ingramcontent.com/pod-product-compliance
Lightning Source LLC
Chambersburg PA
CBHW020458030426
42337CB00011B/143